The Forts
of
Bundelkhand

for
Betwa and Dhruv

Text and Photographs © Rita Sharma ■ Vijai Sharma 2006

First Published 2006
Second Impression 2007

Published by

Rupa ₵ Co

7/16, Ansari Road, Daryaganj
New Delhi - 110 002.

Sales Centres:
Allahabad Bangalooru Chandigarh Chennai
Hyderabad Jaipur Kathmandu
Kolkata Mumbai Pune

Book Design & Typeset by
Seapia Graphics
2204 Sector D2, Vasant Kunj, New Delhi 110 070

Printed in India by
Gopsons Paper Limited
A 14 Sector 16, Noida 201301

The Forts
of
Bundelkhand

TEXT & PHOTOGRAPHS:

RITA SHARMA ■ VIJAI SHARMA

Rupa & Co

CONTENTS

A tribute is due to the local scholar—often, the village *patwari* or teacher—who doubles up as a guide. He has the key to connect events and places for a discourse on Bundelkhand's forts. In this asset, I saw a zeal for promoting preservation and information, reminiscent of the nineteenth century surveyors and officers who rediscovered India and decoded its treasures to piece together the mosaic of heritage we value today.

Years ago, Charles Allen presented me his book *A Glimpse of the Burning Plain—Leaves from the Indian Journals of Charlotte Canning*, noting: 'For Vijai, To remind him that the other side of the story waits to be told'. In this sense, I am not equipped enough. But, in the meanwhile, *The Forts of Bundelkhand* has taken shape. Rita and I have felt fulfilled in writing the book and taking its photographs. We had long wished to do this work on Bundelkhand and feel very happy in being able to do so through Rupa.

A big thank you to our publishers for unhesitatingly agreeing to publish the book. They were understanding and made me feel at ease when I approached them about this project on Bundelkhand, an area quite off the popular circuit. Ms Deepthi Talwar at Rupa has done the editing and so much more; her help was always there, in abundance. Ms Brinda Datta has painstakingly designed the book, and the result is there to see.

At the end of it, one cannot but reflect on the stream of 'calling cards' left behind in Bundelkhand over the millennia, with Kipling:

And the end of the fight is a tombstone white with the name of the late deceased,

And the epitaph drear: 'A Fool lies here who tried to hustle the East'.

In the foreground is our unassailable legacy, kept by the many in Bundelkhand whose forefathers fought alongside the Rani:

Bundele harbolon ke munh hamne suni kahani thee,

Khoob ladi mardani woh to Jhansi wali Rani thee:

From the Bundelkhand folk we heard the story,

Of the brave Jhansi queen, her valour, her glory.

VIJAI SHARMA

Lucknow

Entrance to Jehangir Mahal, Orchha

ACKNOWLEDGEMENTS

❖

Shiv Dayal Trivedi *(for the ever-widening horizons at Jhansi Museum)*
Ranjeet Singh Judeo Samthar
Mukund Lal Mehrotra
Rajeshwar Khare
Rakesh Tewari
Bhagwan Das Gupta
Amita Rajan
Kaushalendra Pratap Yadav
Manoj Maheshwari
Murari Lal Jain
Pramod Kumar Joshi
Shyamanand Upadhyaya
Paritosh Srivastava
Majid Khan Pathan
Om Shankar Khare 'Asar'
Bhagwat Narain Tripathi
Avadhesh Kumar Nigam

State Legislative Library, Lucknow
State Museum, Lucknow
Directorate of U.P. State Archaeology
National Archives of India

An Introduction

This book tells the story of India's heartland. In the bastions and ramparts of the citadels in Bundelkhand is a landscape of events — history, culture and lore — chronicled through letter, thought and song. Time and the elements have taken their toll, but these forts, monumental symbols of our past, continue to survive.

A thousand years ago, the Chandellas defied Mahmud of Ghazni and forced him to accept their terms at Kalinjar. The fort daunted Delhi's formidable Sultan, Sher Shah Sur, who was killed mounting an escalade on its ancient battlements. The echo is still heard of Chhatrasal's horsemen rounding the sal forests at Ajaigarh. And, when Rani Lakshmi Bai rode out of her stronghold at Jhansi to fight the British, a legend was born to inspire an entire national movement.

◀ *Pillared walkways and pavilions of the Bundela fortress-palace at Datia*

▲ *The Orchha complex*

Bundelkhand's historical legacy lies not just in the battles that were fought over it. In art and architecture too, it shone. The symmetry of the pillared walkways and pavilions of the Bundela fortress-palace at Datia sent Edwin Lutyens into raptures, inspiring his designs for New Delhi. Orchha reverberates with the compositions of poet Keshav Das from his *Kavi Priya,* dedicated to Raja Bir Singh's gifted paramour Praveen Rai, who spurned Emperor Jehangir.

Every corner of Bundelkhand has a story. In the coves of Chitrakut, where Lord Rama spent years in exile, the celestial songs of the Ramayana are told and retold amidst the warbling of forest birds. The Deogarh saga is of repose, not of cannon and conquest. Khajuraho's sublime virility has lived through the ages, having survived also the fervour and bigotry of trampling armies on the march from Delhi to the Deccan.

TIMELESS FORTS

India's history of fortifications begins right from the Indus Valley Civilisation. The Harappa citadel, with its barracks, towers and gateways, was encircled by walls of compacted mud and brick. Among the forts in ancient India was the capital of Lord Rama at Ayodhya. The Ramayana also describes the defence system of Lanka as seen by Hanuman. According to the Mahabharata, Hastinapur, the Kaurava capital, and Indraprastha, founded by the Pandavas, were fortified cities.

The Vedas, Puranas and other *shastras* acknowledge the attributes of *giridurga* (hill forts), *jaldurga* (water forts), *mahidurga* (mud forts) and *vanadurga* (forest forts). Caveats are spelt out: the water forts were vulnerable to snakes and the mud forts to rats; the forest forts could be infested by monkeys. The Puranas stipulated the layout, entrance and pathways for function and form, and even the location of elephant houses and cowsheds. Bhishma, in the duties he spells out for rulers in the Mahabharata, stresses on the need for sturdy fort walls, effective patrolling, impregnable moats, secret passages and emergency escapes, vantage archery positions and openings for pouring boiling oil on the enemy.

Kautilya, in his *Arthashastra,* defines the civil and defence administrative linkages in the context of forts. He specifies the location of the treasury and military command in a citadel while elaborating protective mechanisms, keeping in consideration ornamental aspects like lotus-pools, ceremonial arches, esplanades and sacrificial altars. It is evident from the *Smriti-shastras* that lawmakers Manu and Yagnavalkaya influenced a wide range of norms concerning arsenals, medical relief, living areas, kitchens and ladies enclosures. Overall, the evolution of weaponry impacted on the design of fortifications.

THE REGION

Bundelkhand, in central India, is demarcated in the north by the river Yamuna, and extends southward towards the Narmada; the Sindh defines the western limits, and the river Tons, the eastern. A regional melting pot with a distinctive historical and cultural identity, Bundelkhand spreads over southern Uttar Pradesh and northern Madhya Pradesh. The rugged tract of country provided ideal sites for forts, with rocky outcrops and isolated hills rising abruptly from the plains.

The region was called Jajhauti —*Chi-chi-to* for the Chinese — when Hiuen Tsang came to India in the seventh century. Some 400 years later, Alberuni, accompanying Mahmud of Ghazni, referred to Jajhauti and Khajuraho. Ibn Batutah, the fourteenth century traveller from Tangier in Morocco, also visited the region, including Khajuraho and Chanderi. According to Alexander Cunningham, the first head of the Indian Archaeological Survey, Jajhauti corresponded with Bundelkhand, as the region later came to be known.

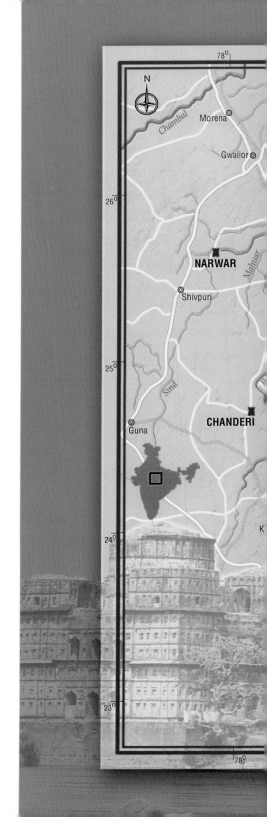

FORTS OF BUNDELKHAND

OUDH

Pandu

Auraiya

Kanpur
Unnao

Yamuna

Jalaun

Kalpi

Sai

Pratapgarh

Orai
Betwa
Hamirpur

Fatehpur

SAMTHAR

awali

Erich

U T T A R   P R A D E S H

Ganga

Dhasan

Ken

Garara

Yamuna

KUNDAR

CHARKHARI

Banda

Allahabad

BARWASAGAR

Baghan

MAHOBA

Mau

KALINJAR

Belan

AJAIGARH

Khajuraho

Tons

BAGHELKHAND

Panna

Satna

Rewa

Son

Maihar

Katni

DHAMONI

M A D H Y A   P R A D E S H

Murwara

ar

Damoh

Sihora

	Forts
◎	Other Places
—	Main Road
—	Other Road
⋯	Railways
	River

Jabalpur

0   20
KM

79°   80°   81°   82°

26°

25°

24°

23°

THE EARLY RULERS

In pre-historical times, indigenous tribes inhabited the wooded tracts in Bundelkhand. The earliest Aryans in these parts were the Chedis. Their kingdom Chedirashtra was among the principal domains in the sixth century BC. It appears that Chedibhukti — *bhukti* is the equivalent of province — became Jejakabhukti, or in its shorter version, Jajhauti. The region saw the rule of the Nandas, Mauryans, Sungas, Kushanas, Nagas and the Guptas.

Samudragupta was the dominant power in the fourth century AD. The Hun invasions towards the close of the fifth century hastened the Gupta decline. A relic of the late Gupta period in Bundelkhand is the Vishnu temple at Deogarh. Harshvardhana held part of the region in the first half of the seventh century, co-existing with other rulers at various levels of dependency. In the forest-clad low hills, the Gonds held sway. The Pratihara Rajputs were ascendant in the eighth century. They ruled from Kannauj.

◀ *Carvings at the Vishnu temple, Deogarh – a Gupta period legacy*

▶ *Anantsayi Vishnu panel in the Deogarh temple*

THE CHANDELLAS

An influential dynasty, the Chandellas were once tributaries of the Pratiharas. During the ninth century, the Chandellas eclipsed their overlords in Bundelkhand: a mutually sapping struggle with the Deccan Rashtrakutas weakened the Pratiharas, enabling the Chandellas to break away and dominate the region for 300 years. The Chandella fall was precipitous, accelerated by a debilitating rivalry with Prithviraj Chauhan of Delhi. The final blow was the ransacking of the Chandella administrative capital Mahoba by Qutub-ud-din Aibak, founder of the Delhi Sultanate.

The Chandellas became a shadow of their former self, withdrawing into their strongholds at Kalinjar and Ajaigarh. Centuries later, a Chandella star appeared: Durgavati of Gondwana. Married into the Gonds, she was the daughter of the Chandella chief of Kalinjar, Kirat Singh. He was executed when the fort fell — even as the victor, Sher Shah

▲ *The Chandellas were renowned builders: temples at Khajuraho*

◀ *Chandella reservoir and water system, Kalinjar*

▲ *Carvings on the rock face near the Neel Kantha temple, Kalinjar – various icons of the Brahminical faith*

Sur, succumbed to his battle wounds. Some years after, Durgavati perished defending Gondwana against Akbar.

The Chandellas, it is surmised, were indigenous people. Legend links the Chandellas to the lunar race, the Chandravanshis. The first in line was Chandravarman, born of Hemavati, daughter of the Brahmin priest of the Raja of Kashi. According to legend, a smitten moon-god, Chandrama, embraced the beautiful Hemavati. She conceived and thus was born the Chandella dynasty.

Chandella ingenuity was strikingly demonstrated in the temples at Khajuraho and the irrigation systems built by the dynasty that helped to sustain large semi-arid areas. A millennium later, the Viceroy, Lord Curzon, borrowed a leaf from the Chandellas when he decided to dam the streams in the region to irrigate the poor soil.

▲ *View of the Chaturbhuj Temple, Orchha*

THE BUNDELAS

The Bundela Rajputs were Suryavanshis. Legend has it that a local Gaharwar Rajput chief did tireless penance to appease the goddess Vindhyavasini Devi at her abode on the Vindhyan range. The chief cut off his own head as an offering. A satisfied *devi* accorded the blessing that the drop or *boond* of blood — suggestive of 'Boondela' or 'Bundela' — falling on the sacrificial altar would yield great rulers. It is said also that 'Vindhyela' was the name given to the lineage, which over time was altered to 'Bundela'.

There are accounts that the Bundelas branched off from the Kannauj Pratihara dynasty. This offshoot had come in control of Kashi. The Bundela chief had three sons. The eldest, Hemkaran, was the ablest, but the other two brothers conspired to get him expelled from Kashi. Hemkaran propitiated the *devi* and settled near present-day Banda. His successors ruled from Mahoni for two centuries.

In the thirteenth century, the Bundelas had to contend with the Khangars, who ruled from Kundar. Vrindavan Lal Verma's *Garh Kundar* is an account of the ebb and tide of this dynasty's fortunes. The Khangars — former vassals of the Chandellas — were outwitted and wiped out by the Bundelas in what became a bloody culmination of a wedding ceremony. Kundar became the Bundela capital. The aftermath of Timur's invasion, towards the end of the fourteenth century, allowed the Bundelas a freer run in the region.

▲ *Jehangir Mahal, Orchha*

THE MUGHALS

The Bundela shift from Kundar to a more sheltered Orchha in the sixteenth century was influenced by the region's growing vulnerability to the Mughals. Babar had taken Kalpi and Chanderi. Akbar, who transformed a kingdom into an empire, kept up the pressure after annexing Gwalior.

It was early in the seventeenth century that a Bundela–Mughal fusion of interests took place, triggered by the murder of Akbar's trusted counsellor, Abul Fazl. The assassin was Orchha's Bir Singh; the crime was perpetrated to further the interests of Prince Salim who soon became the Emperor Jehangir. Bir Singh exploited his proximity with the seat of power for the benefit of the Bundela Rajputs.

The late seventeenth and early eighteenth centuries in Bundelkhand belonged to the flamboyant Chhatrasal of Panna. His defiance of Delhi's imperial authority and protracted conflict with the Mughal satraps led to the entry of the Marathas in Bundelkhand. The incursions of the Mughal governor of Farrukhabad, Bangash Khan, into Chhatrasal's dominions, compelled the Bundelas to invite Maratha help from Peshwa Baji Rao I.

▶ *Detail of a miniature painting depicting Mughal Emperor Jehangir receiving an assembly at Agra. Prince Khurram (Shahjehan) and his son Shuja are also seen*

THE MARATHAS

The Peshwa's troops trounced Bangash Khan. Having gained access into Bundelkhand, the Marathas stayed on. An ageing Chhatrasal, under pressure, found it prudent to will part of his possessions to the Peshwa, who expanded in Bundelkhand. Nauru Shankar was the first Peshwa-appointed *subehdar* in Jhansi. The defeat at Panipat of the next Peshwa, Balaji Baji Rao, by the Afghans was a shock to the Marathas, but they recovered soon. Even when retreating from Panipat, the Marathas were able to marshal resources enough to plunder Bundela territory.

The Peshwa's protégés were aggressive. A favourite buccaneer was the Nawab of Banda, Ali Bahadur, whose father was the son of Baji Rao I from the concubine Mastani — she had been

gifted to the Maratha chief by a deeply indebted Chhatrasal. The Mughals were declining rapidly now. Delhi, as the centre, had ceased to hold. This state of affairs was confirmed when the Mughal Emperor Shah Alam's eyes were gouged out in his own palace in the Red Fort by a treasure-hunting Rohilla brigand, Ghulam Kadir, who himself met a blood-curdling end at the hands of Mahadji Scindia.

◄ *A statue of Peshwa Baji Rao I, who established Maratha power in Bundelkhand, in Pune*

► *Seat of the Mughul Emperor in the Red Fort, Delhi*

THE BRITISH

The blinded Mughal continued to reign — the British were amenable to this. The Scindia treated the remains of the Mughal empire as part of the Maratha protectorate. The charade of a Mughal emperor on the throne suited the British, who bided time — their intervention always on call, more so since the cessation of Anglo-French hostilities in India at the end of Europe's Seven Years War. The reign of Shah Alam and his two successors limped on, before the great uprising of 1857 swept away the Mughals.

The Marathas, dominant between the *doab* and the Deccan, increasingly came into conflict with the British. This was in the backdrop of the Mughal collapse. The chiefs in Bundelkhand, apprehensive of the Marathas, drew closer to the British. Chhatrasal's descendants bound themselves to the British with promise of allegiance and fidelity in return for *sanads* — deeds — confirming possession of their hereditary lands. Separately, the rulers of Orchha, Datia and Samthar entered into treaty relations of cordiality and mutual assistance with the British.

▲ *A memorial stone at Jhansi*

▲ *The Rani of Jhansi in battle – detail of a miniature painting, Bundelkhand School of Art (nineteenth century)*

1857

The Anglo-Maratha wars led to the Peshwa's exile from Pune. He settled in Bithoor, not far from the northern fringes of Bundelkhand. The Maratha sun had set with the British acquiring territorial rights in the region from the Peshwa. But the churning, which led to the momentous events of 1857, returned the Marathas to the frontline under Nana Sahib, the adopted son of the exiled Peshwa. Maratha and Bundela were pitted against each other. The pivot of the uprising in Bundelkhand was the Rani of Jhansi. From here commenced the chiselling of a new nation.

Jhansi

Jhansi fort rises above the rock-strewn plains, a monument to the indomitable spirit of Rani Lakshmi Bai. Dead leaves rustle on the mottled stone, grey or glowing according to the time of the day. The wind sighs softly. The silent graves on the fort's deserted terraces yield themselves to the elements, oblivious to the bustle of the town below.

The Raja of Jhansi was Gangadhar Rao. His wife had died and he was childless. In 1842, the Raja married Manikarnika, the daughter of Moropant Tambe, a retainer of Chimanji Appa, the exiled Peshwa Baji Rao II's brother. The girl was given a new name, Lakshmi Bai. Her father, also a widower, was persuaded to settle down in Jhansi. The Raja got Moropant married again to a woman called Chimnabai.

When Lakshmi Bai's newborn son died in 1851, the need arose to identify a successor to Gangadhar Rao. The British, as the paramount power, were ratifying successions and pertinent family adoptions under Governor-General Lord Dalhousie's (1848-56) Doctrine of Lapse —

▶ *Miniature painting depicting Lakshmi Bai, Rani of Jhansi*

essentially, an instrument of annexation. Gangadhar Rao, before his death in 1853, adopted a son named Damodar Rao, to circumvent the British from taking over Jhansi for want of a successor. But, it was to no avail.

Dalhousie's view was that the Jhansi chief had not been a ruler; he was only the Peshwa's *subehdar*, or administrative head of a province. With the Peshwa extinguished, his possessions in Bundelkhand, including Jhansi, would have to lapse into British India. Soon, the tumult of 1857 would bring the fort at Jhansi to the centre stage.

In fact, Jhansi's story begins much earlier. In the seventeenth century, it was part of the Orchha kingdom. In 1602, Bir Singh, a younger brother of the Orchha ruler, waylaid and murdered Akbar's friend and chief counsellor, Abul Fazl. The deed was perpetrated at the behest of Salim, son of the emperor. The headstrong prince, estranged from his father, had hated Abul Fazl — 'the

▲ *The main gate to the Jhansi fort*

King's Jonathan' (Smith, 2004, p 360). When Salim succeeded as Emperor Jehangir (1605–27), he conferred Orchha on Bir Singh. The hillock across the Betwa appeared to Bir Singh as a *jhainsi*, a reflection, and he ordered a fort to be built there.

▲ *A pleasure garden inside the Jhansi fort*

Stone-cutters and masons sweated in Jhansi's heat to raise this fort of native stone. The spot was occupied from much earlier, as borne out by the Chandella pillars and stone slabs embedded in the fort. The outer defence, contouring the city of over four miles circumference, was a fortified wall of a height varying from eighteen to thirty feet, and with a thickness of six to twelve feet. There were ten gates: Baragaon, Bhander, Datia, Jhirna, Khanderao, Lakshmi, Orchha, Sagar, Sainyar and Unnao, with a number of *khirkis* or smaller entrances.

The fort was being held by Vasant Singh — appointed its keeper by the Orchha ruler Jujhar Singh — when it was captured in 1634 by the Mughal general Makramat Khan, along with its well-stocked granary, artillery, a powder magazine and treasury. This seizure was ordered by Emperor Shahjehan (1628–58) because of his antagonism towards Jujhar Singh, dating to the time when both were princes. The Mughals handed over the fort to a Bundela chief, Girdhar, for maintenance on their behalf. It was restored to Orchha when the Bundela-Mughal relationship normalised.

Early in the eighteenth century, Jhansi came under the sway of Chhatrasal of Panna who pillaged Mughal territory. In reaction, Bundelkhand was invaded by the Mughal governor of Farrukhabad. In 1729, Chhatrasal, now eighty, enlisted Maratha help and the intruders were expelled. A relieved Chhatrasal greeted Peshwa Baji Rao I as his son. This was signal for an

avaricious Peshwa to claim a share of Chhatrasal's domains in parity with the Bundela's two sons in line for inheritance. Chhatrasal, reluctantly, willed one-third of his possessions, including Jhansi, to the Peshwa.

The Maratha phase in Jhansi commenced with Nauru Shankar as the Peshwa's *subehdar* (1742–57). The fortifications were improved, a triple wall came up and the water supply was augmented. Shankargarh was the new wing, named after a Shiva temple. Despite the area's poor agricultural productivity, a town flourished in the fort vicinity with cotton trading as an important economic activity. Tax collection was robust.

The Maratha-held fort of Jhansi was seized by the Nawab of Oudh, Shuja-ud-daulah, in 1762. The pretext came when the Marathas invaded Mughal territory administered by the Nawab, who continued nominally to be the viceroy of a rapidly declining emperor in Delhi. The Marathas recaptured Jhansi in 1766, for which the Holkar of Indore provided leadership and resources.

Jhansi was coveted by the Jats of Bharatpur and Mathura, and also by the Afghan Rohillas from the upper Gangetic plains east of Delhi. They were outmanoeuvred by Jhansi's *subehdar* Raghunath Rao Nevalkar (1769–96), who was an able administrator and reformer of the revenue system. He abdicated in favour of his brother Sheo Rao Bhao (1796–1814) and took *jal samadhi* in Kashi. Later chiefs cosied up to the British to promote their individual standing independent of the Peshwa.

Ramchandra Rao (1814–35), the next chief, was a grandson of Sheo Rao Bhao. He helped the British in the Anglo-Burmese war and the siege of Bharatpur. The Governor-General, Lord Amherst (1823–28), sent him a robe of honour and a letter in appreciation of his assistance.

Ramchandra Rao assumed the title of 'Raja' with British approval. He was also conferred an appellation, Maharajadhiraj Fidvi Badshah Jamjah Inglistan, or 'devoted servant of the glorious King of England' by Governor-General Lord Bentinck (1828–35), who visited Jhansi in 1832.

Jhansi's amity with the British suffered after the departure of Bentinck, who was oriented more towards social reforms than aggressive politics. Jhansi soon became vulnerable to British manipulations. The new chief Raghunath Rao (1835–38), afflicted by leprosy, left the task of administration to others. The succession claims following his death gave the British an opening to intervene. In the fray were Raghunath Rao's brother Gangadhar Rao, an issueless wife and an illegitimate son from a Muslim concubine.

The British appointed Gangadhar Rao as chief (1842–53). He took over from a stopgap Court of Wards administered by the British political agent in Bundelkhand. The series of travails regarding succession in Jhansi weighed against Gangadhar Rao getting the status of a ruling

▲ *The exterior face of the Rani Mahal, the residence of Lakshmi Bai*

▲ *Painted walls and ceilings of rooms in Rani Mahal*

chief. Earlier too, Sheo Rao Bhau, manoeuvred by a dead son's widow, had opted for an infant grandson, Ramchandra Rao — the widow's son — to succeed him, over and above his two sons Raghunath Rao and Gangadhar Rao from another wife. Dalhousie's policies, as designed, led to Jhansi's annexation or 'lapse' into British India following Gangadhar Rao's death and the absence of a natural heir.

Lakshmi Bai was pensioned off. She lived modestly, as evident from the unpretentious motifs which remain in her residence. Adornments like fancy gargoyles and patterned columns were few, though the palace walls coated with *kauri* paste still retain their creaminess despite the flaking and discolouration that have taken place over the years. There were trees and leisure-swings, and occasion for the Rani to experiment with perfumes and *ittar* in the pavilions and courtyards of the fort and the Rani Mahal.

The Rani had a stabilising influence, which muffled unrest following the annexation. Public disquiet came from a conviction that the British were in the wrong. Captain W.H. Sleeman, architect of the *thugee* eradication campaign and also a personal friend of Raja Ramchandra Rao, had said (1915, p 221):

'I have always considered Jhansi among the native states of Bundelkhand as a kind of oasis in the desert, the only one in which a man can accumulate property with the confidence of being permitted by its rulers freely to display and enjoy it.'

When the uprising was sparked of in 1857, the garrison and cavalry detachment in Jhansi sympathised with it. Arson was widespread and many officers were killed. The atmosphere was particularly charged due to the removal of the ban on cow slaughter, the belief that the new Enfield cartridges were smeared with animal fat and a rumour that flour was mixed with ground animal bones.

from sixteen to twenty feet…has extensive and elaborate outworks of the same solid construction, with front and flanking embrasures for artillery-fire, and loop-holes, of which, in some places, there were five tiers, for musketry.'

(*Freedom Struggle in Uttar Pradesh*, Vol III, 1959, p 326)

When the engagement came in April 1858, the Rani was in full gear on horseback, riding across the fort amidst the cannon roar and volleys of bullets. British batteries rained fire for seventeen days. The Rani's troops returned fire vigorously from the high walls, well endowed for mounting artillery. The citizenry was on hand, helping with food, buckets of water to control fires and fixing the breaches. According to Hugh Rose:

'The Chief of the Rebel artillery was a first-rate Artillery man; he had under him two Companies…The manner in which the Rebels served their guns, repaired their defences, and reopened fire from Batteries and guns repeatedly shut up, was remarkable. From some Batteries they returned shot for shot. The women were seen working in the Batteries and carrying ammunition. The garden Battery was fought under the black flag of the Fakeers…Everything indicated a determined resistance .'

(*Freedom Struggle in Uttar Pradesh*, Vol III, 1959, p 328)

An attack on a gunpowder dump in the fort caused irreparable damage — traitors had reported the vulnerable points to the enemy. The Rani, deeply religious, knelt on the ramparts and prayed to Goddess Durga. She scanned the distant hillocks for the expected arrival of Tatya Tope and his 20,000-strong reinforcement. The priest invoked Lord Ganesha in the fort temple. But Tatya's army, intercepted at Barwasagar twelve miles away, had fled in disarray after a pitched battle.

Relentless enemy cannon caused a breach in the city wall between the Sainyar and Jhirna gates. Undaunted, the Rani supervised the repairs. But the damage widened due to the cannonade. The defenders mentally steeled themselves to stand ground and fight to the last. There was savage hand-to-hand fighting in the streets. After a spirited defence, the city walls gave way and enemy troops poured in.

The town was now burning. Advisers persuaded the Rani to leave the fort. She climbed down from a turret window with Damodar Rao on her back and rode off in the darkness to Kalpi.

◀ *The Ganesh Temple inside the Jhansi fort*

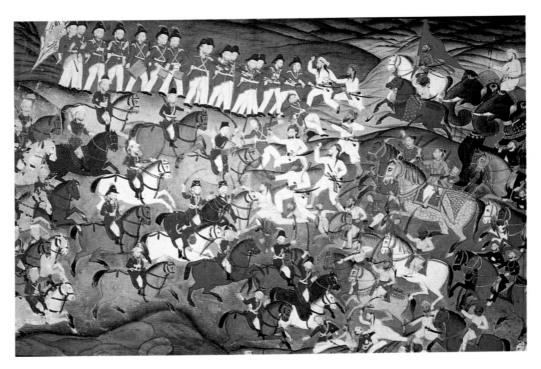

▲ *A miniature painting depicting the Rani of Jhansi in battle against the British*

Pursuers were cut down in close combat. Cornet Combe, of the 3rd Bombay Light Cavalry, recorded:

> 'We were sent all over the country in pursuit, and one of our troops overtook her... Her escort made a hard fight of it, and though our fellows did their utmost and killed every man, she got away, her smart saddle falling into our hands. She is a wonderful woman, very brave and determined. It is fortunate for us that the men are not all like her.' (Hibbert, 1978, p 383)

Nana Sahib and Tatya Tope met up with the Rani at Kalpi. They marched to Gwalior and took the fort. Scindia's army joined the revolutionaries. Hugh Rose gave pursuit. It was a blistering June summer of 1858, when a fierce fight took place near Gwalior. Lakshmi Bai was killed — shot and run through with a sabre. She was dressed as a man 'using her sword with both hands and holding the reins of her horse in her mouth'. (Hibbert, 1978, p 385) Hugh Rose recognised her to be 'the bravest and best military leader of the rebels'. (Edwardes, 1963, p 186)

Those from Lakshmi Bai's troops who were captured were hanged or blown away by cannon. Jhansi town was sacked. Moropant Tambe, the Rani's father, was apprehended in Datia, brought to Jhansi and hanged. His wife Chimnabai managed to get out of the fort and walk unnoticed across fields to her father's house forty miles away. Damodar Rao was whisked away and remained in hiding before being allowed to settle in Holkar's Indore. Time passed. Damodar Rao's wedding was attended by Chimnabai. Her son from Moropant became a tehsildar in British Sagar. Hugh Rose was titled 'Baron Straithnairn of Straithnairn and of Jhansi'; he spent his last days in Paris.

In 1861, the British handed over the fort to the Scindia as part of an administrative protocol that included exchange of villages and other assets to adjust for the expenses incurred during the recent events. The fort was returned to the British in 1886. Repairs were undertaken, pathways paved, gates and railings added and new walls raised.

Today, the fort shows up as two back-to-back architectural entities, Indian and British, indifferent to each other. There is the verdure of a past and silence in the fort. The Rani's figure, clad in battle attire, stares from many a monument, painting and sculpture. The battles she lost are victories. The citadel at Jhansi conveys the aura of a great historic event. It is a symbol of triumph.

THE FORTS OF BUNDELKHAND

Orchha

Across the sparkling Betwa and the sun-drenched green of the dhak forests, the lofty Orchha fortress-palaces and temples silhouette the skyline. Every curve and contour of the magnificent edifices at Orchha displays the headiness of its rulers who combined the best of Rajput and Mughal styles.

Orchha was a picturesque spot. When Bundela ruler Rudra Pratap (1501–31) chanced upon it during a hunt, he decided to shift his capital from Kundar to Orchha. The new location for the capital was also safer. Rudra Pratap had held well against the Lodi Sultans, but with the Mughals having gained entry, Bundelkhand was vulnerable. However, before he could actually make the move, Rudra Pratap died in an attempt to save a cow from a tiger. It was left to Rudra Pratap's sons, Bharati Chand (1531–54) and Madhukar Shah (1554–92), to fulfil their father's vision for Orchha.

Soon after their shift, the Mughal emperor Akbar (1556–1605), after annexing Gwalior, turned to Bundelkhand. The Orchha forces proved to be too strong initially. The terrain was difficult, thick with jungle and without open pathways. The Mughals had to fortify their campaign and put into battle a coalition including the Kachhwahas of Narwar. Madhukar Shah lost a son, Haural Dev, and the Bundelas were finally forced to capitulate to the Mughal general, Sadiq Khan. However, a stubborn Madhukar Shah refused to bow down before his conqueror.

Madhukar's obduracy manifested when he wore a huge vermilion foot-shaped *tilak* in the form of God's *charan* in Akbar's presence, disregarding the code on headmarks such as these prevalent in the Mughal court. However, the emperor could not bring himself to chastise the Orchha king for what came to be known as the 'Madhukar Shahi Tilak'. The Bundela chief also ignored Akbar's call to accompany the Mughal campaign in the Deccan, and did not make the

▲ *The entrance to Jehangir Mahal*

The Betwa waterfront with chhatries of rulers

▲ *The western face of Jehangir Mahal*

customary courtesy visit when the emperor's son Murad was appointed Malwa's governor. Undeviating till his last days, Madhukar Shah died aged eighty in the Narwar forests, while retreating from an engagement with the imperial troops.

Orchha went into a decline after Madhukar's son Ram Shah (1592–1605) succeeded. The ruler was unable to cope with the ambitions of collaterals and open rebellious activity by a number of brothers, including Bir Singh. A son, Sangram Shah, was killed in Erich trying to capture Bir Singh, then a fugitive from Akbar. When Jehangir succeeded (1605–27), he deposed Ram Shah and gave the throne of Orchha to Bir Singh.

This was the new emperor's compensation to Bir Singh for assassinating the scholar-statesman Abul Fazl at his bidding when he was still Prince Salim, and yet to ascend the throne as Jehangir. Salim had believed that Abul Fazl was poisoning Akbar's ears against him. At the prince's behest,

Bir Singh waylaid Abul Fazl near Narwar as he returned to Agra from the Deccan, after being summoned by an anxious emperor, Akbar, for consultations. Bir Singh, with 500 horsemen, ambushed and killed Abul Fazl, severed his head and sent it to Salim, then residing in Allahabad fort.

With Bir Singh (1605–27) on the throne, Orchha's fortunes were restored. The Bundela maintained a closeness with Jehangir. He assisted the Mughal general Mahabat Khan to ensure the submission of Mewar, and later joined up with the imperial forces for the Emperor's Deccan operations. This led to the elevation of the Orchha military officials by the emperor. Jehangir also asked Bir Singh to accompany his son — the inexperienced Prince Khurram — on an expedition to Udaipur.

Bir Singh was a compulsive builder. Apart from the Jehangir Mahal, he built the Lakshmi Narayan temple, the Datia fortress-palace, *dharmashalas* and irrigation tanks. Much gold was donated to the Mathura temples. But Bir Singh could be forbidding: he ordered a public trial for a son, Jagat Dev, accused of setting hunting dogs on a sadhu who was mauled fatally. Jagat Dev was condemned to be bitten to death by dogs.

Bir Singh was succeeded by Jujhar Singh (1627–34). Shahjehan's animosity towards Jujhar dated back to the time when he, as Prince Khurram, had revolted against his father Jehangir. The Emperor had given the task of quelling this rebellion to Bir Singh, who in turn had handed the responsibility of heading a 1000-horse army to Jujhar Singh. After Khurram became emperor, Jujhar Singh paid him the formal visit of a tributary, but this did not smoothen relations between the two: Shahjehan felt slighted when the Bundela made a quiet exit despite an invitation to stay on for the celebrations at Agra.

There was vehement opposition from Jujhar Singh when Shahjehan imposed fresh taxes. He was suspected also to have connived in the safe passage of the rebel Khan Jehan Lodi through Orchha territory. Eventually Jujhar Singh gave in and went with the Mughals to the Deccan. However, on the journey back, the tempestuous Jujhar Singh attacked the Gonds, ignoring Shahjehan's caveat not to press on with the operations. The Gond chief Prem Narayan was killed and considerable treasure fell into Bundela hands.

Shahjehan ordered the return of the Gond possessions and deposit of a portion of the plunder in the imperial treasury. He despatched his son Aurangzeb to take on an unwilling Jujhar Singh. The Mughal prince stormed Orchha. The Bundela escaped, taking the women from his *zenana* and whatever wealth he could deep into Bundelkhand to the forest fort of Dhamoni. But he was captured by the Gonds and brutally killed along with his son. The emperor then installed Devi Singh of Chanderi at Orchha (1634–36).

When Shahjehan visited Orchha, the architecture invoked his envy and many buildings were torched. There was a move for mass conversions, which invoked a reaction from the Bundela

jagirdars. Devi Singh fled back to Chanderi. Anarchy ruled till Shahjehan assigned Pahar Singh (1641–53), a brother of Jujhar Singh, to the throne. He ran some successful campaigns against the Gonds under the Mughals. Orchha's position recovered, followed by victories against Chauragarh and Raisen forts, south of Bundelkhand.

Pahar Singh accompanied Prince Murad Baksh, Shahjehan's son, to the harsh Balkh campaign and in the operations in Kabul and Kandahar against the Persians. His successor, Sujan Singh (1653–72), went with the Mughals to Kashmir, Bijapur and Cooch Behar. Aurangzeb (1658–1707) also deputed Sujan Singh to go on an expedition to Shivaji's Purandar fort.

With the Mughals going into a steep decline in the closing years of Aurangzeb's reign, Udot Singh (1689–1736) came to rule over Orchha; he was the contemporary of six Mughal emperors in Delhi. Udot Singh kept up with the shifting imperial priorities and participated in the Mughal campaign against the Sikhs.

Panna's star had simultaneously risen under the indefatigable Chhatrasal (b.1649, d.1731), who was determined to erase Mughal presence from Bundelkhand. Chhatrasal, originally a fief-holder of Orchha, had met Chhatrapati Shivaji (b.1627, d.1680) in his early days. The Maratha motivated the Bundela to chart out a course that would give him freedom from the Mughals.

Orchha's energies were now directed to keeping at bay Chhatrasal, and later, as the eighteenth century wore on, the Marathas. Getting out of the Maratha route to the *doab* became a priority.

▲ *A courtyard inside Jehangir Mahal*

The capital was shifted from Orchha to Tikamgarh in 1783 during the rule of Vikramajit (1776–1817). Orchha also established relations with the British through a treaty in 1812.

Orchha was the premier Bundela state. The assimilation of Mughal styles in Bundelkhand's architecture is reflected in the Jehangir Mahal built by Bir Singh in the early seventeenth century. The square-shaped palace is a sprawling construction, 220 feet on each side. The facade is richly decorated, with imposing arcades and large fluted domes, and sandstone walls adorned with designs and geometric patterns. The entrance portal, flanked by sculpted elephants and embroidered with cusped arches, leads to a spacious interior.

The Betwa can be seen through a delicate lattice on the screen windows of the Jehangir Mahal. Light plays in lively reflection on the shell-plastered walls of a three-storeyed set of pavilions profusely decorated with blossoms, tendrils and arabesques. The eaves and piers are overlaid with

▲ *The Raj Mahal built by Orchha's founder Rudra Pratap and his sons*

▲ *Wall paintings in Raj Mahal*

lace work. The walls have depictions of *Ras Lila* — dramas or performances based on Lord Krishna, Radha and the *gopis*. Elephant brackets support a russet cornice, which runs along the periphery enclosing a courtyard with a fountain in the centre.

Construction on the Raj Mahal was started by Rudra Pratap — Orchha's founder — and completed by Bharati Chand. This sixteenth-century building housed the administrative secretariat and the *diwankhana*. Closely-woven wall paintings depict the Vishnu *dasavataras*, the *apsaras* and mythological scenes from Anantsayi Vishnu and Varaha rescuing the world. The drama, depictions of which range from the subdued and pastel to the gaudy and strident, unfolds in the mellowness of the interior apartments.

The colossal Chaturbhuj temple was built over a fifteen-year period by an intensely god-fearing Madhukar Shah in the late sixteenth century. The temple has no parallel. With its conical shikharas and lofty ceilings, the structure is audacious, appearing more like a medieval cathedral than a traditional temple. Clearly, Bundela temple architecture in Orchha had come a long way from the dark narrow sanctums and closed *antaralas* of Chandella Khajuraho.

The spacious interiors of the Orchha temples reflect Hindu renaissance. The Bhakti cult influenced worship rituals and, consequently, the architecture of the shrines. Congregational worship altered temple interiors, from the confines reserved for priests and the chosen few, to spacious halls for accommodating large numbers of devotees.

The Laxmi Narayan temple built by Bir Singh is embroidered with Hindu mythology and battle scenes. Other buildings include the elegant Sheesh Mahal and Phool Bagh palace complex, which was refurbished later for European guests. Redstone columns supported a spacious audience hall. The palace was kept cool by a conduit-network connected to water towers. Terraces and pavilions overlook Mughal-style gardens with geometrical patterns interspersed with water canals.

Dwarfed by the Chaturbhuj temple is the Ram Raja temple: squat, sprawling and white washed. The temple was built as a palace by Madhukar Shah for his wife Ganesh Kunwar. Her deity was Rama — his was Krishna. Legend has it that the Rani prayed to Rama at Ayodhya by the river Saryu. She was blessed by Rama, who promised to return with her to Orchha. The condition was that the Rani walk the 250-mile journey back with an idol of Rama, which once lodged, was not to be removed. Rama was to live in Orchha like a raja.

▶ *The Chaturbhuj temple built by Madhukar Shah*

◀ The Laxmi Narayan temple, built by Bir Singh, renovated in late eighteenth century

The Rani took eight months to return to Orchha. But the temple for Rama was not complete and the deity had to be placed in the Rani's palace. After the Chaturbhuj temple was built, attempts were made to shift the idol of Rama to its new home. However, it refused to budge from its place; no one could move it. Subsequently, an image of Vishnu was installed in the temple meant for Rama, and the Rani's palace became the Ram Raja temple. The Ram Navami festival is still celebrated with fervour in Orchha.

A symbol of sacrifice in Orchha is the *samadhi* of Jujhar Singh's younger brother Hardaul. Jujhar suspected his wife and Hardaul of having intimate relations. He ordered his wife to poison Hardaul. The Rani, devoted to her husband and grieved at the insinuation, did not offer Hardaul the poisoned meal as directed. The interests of his *bhabhi* were supreme for Hardaul: he ate the meal and died. This sacrifice is commemorated in Bundelkhand villages, where houses have a Hardaul-ka-chabutra, or platform where Hardaul is venerated as a minor deity.

The Orchha rulers patronised literature. Here lived the great poet Keshav Das (b.1555, d.1617), author of *Vigyan Gita,* dedicated to Madhukar Shah. His *Kavi Priya* prescribes the traits of poetry and his *Ram Chandrika* is among the finest

▶ The Samadhi of Hardaul

▲ *A panoramic view of Raj Mahal at Orchha – the Bundela spirit lives on*

popular verses in Hindi. Other works by Keshav are *Rasik Priya*, a book on poetry composition, and *Ram Alankritmanjari*, on prosody. Keshav was influential enough to prevail upon Birbal, one of Akbar's 'nine jewels', to obtain the exoneration of a fine imposed by the emperor on a son of Madhukar Shah for a misdemeanour. Bir Singh's mistress, Praveen Rai, was an accomplished poet too.

Today, the Bundela spirit lives on in the magnificence of the fortress-palace complex at Orchha. The town itself appears sleepy and shrunken today, encircled by old city walls like an oversized garment. Turrets, domes and spires are everywhere. And in the pearly shadows, it is difficult to tell where reality ends and illusion begins.

Datia

A tiara of cupolas and chhatries crowns the gigantic fortress-palace of Datia. Rising from the bedrock, the citadel towers over a lake, embodying in its resplendence, the freewheeling spirit of the builder, Bir Singh.

The uniformity and symmetry of Mughal-style architecture is combined with Hindu form, ornamental designs and motifs. Captain Sleeman, during a visit in 1835, was enraptured by the beauty of Datia; and as his guide reflected (1915, p 237):

'The noble works in palaces and temples, which you see around you, Sir, mouldering in ruins, were built by princes who had beaten emperors in battle, and whose spirits still hover over and protect the place…, when hostile forces…threatened…spirits of men like Bir Singh Deo and Hardaul Lala…had come to our aid.'

The Datia fortress-palace is believed to have been financed largely from the treasure that Bir Singh looted from Abul Fazl after killing him on the request of Jehangir when he was a prince. Bir Singh's loyalty towards his patron Jehangir never wavered. In 1625, when the emperor was seized by Mahabat Khan on his way to Kabul, prompt aid was forthcoming from Bir Singh. He sent Bhagwan Rao, one of his twelve sons, to the emperor's aid.

▶ *The Datia fortress-palace built by Bir Singh and financed by the loot from Abul Fazl*

Bir Singh carved out a *jagir*, Palera, for Bhagwan Rao. However, family strife saw Bhagwan Rao shut out of Palera by the sons of his younger wife when he returned from an expedition. Bir Singh intervened. He bestowed Datia on Bhagwan Rao to nip any escalation of bad blood.

Bhagwan Rao further cemented his relationship with the Mughals when the Pathan nobleman Khan Jehan Lodi, Governor of the Deccan, rebelled against the recently ascended Shahjehan. Lodi supported Dawar Baksh — son of the new emperor's late half-brother Prince Khusro — a rival contender to the imperial throne. Bhagwan Rao joined the Mughal army to fight the rebel. The Bundela chief lost a brother, Nahar Singh, in battle. After the rebels were subdued, Bhagwan Rao became part of the Mughal campaign in Bijapur (1631).

James Todd, the British political agent in Rajputana wrote:

'From the period of Akbar the Boondelas bore a distinguished part in all the grand conflicts, to the very close of the monarchy: nor among all the brave chiefs of Rajasthan, did any perform more gallant or faithful services than the Boondela chieftains of Orcha and Duttea.

Bagwan commanded the advanced guard of the army of Shahjehan. His son, Soopkurna, was Aurangzebe's most distinguished leader in the Dekhan.' (1978, p 97)

Bhagwan Rao also helped suppress a revolt by the Lahore Governor, paving the way for Shahjehan's first visit to the city in 1634. In return, a *mansab*, lands, and gifts were conferred on the Datia chief. The chronic tension between the Mughals and Orchha's Jujhar Singh — a step-brother of Bhagwan Rao — led to a situation enabling Datia to consolidate its own position. Bhagwan Rao, with his kinsman Devi Singh of Chanderi, assisted the Mughals in hunting down Jujhar Singh after his rebellion. Bhagwan Rao's cenotaph, the *suraahi chhatri*, still stands near the town.

The military tradition continued with Shubhkaran (1656–83), successor of Bhagwan Rao. By now, Datia had enough standing to snap the umbilical cord with Orchha and shape its own space under the Mughals. Delhi's war of succession (1657–59) had Datia on Aurangzeb's winning side, though Shubhkaran lost a half-brother, Prithviraj, in battle. Shubhkaran fought at Samugarh (1658) where Dara Shikoh, eldest of Shahjehan's four contending sons, was defeated, and at Khajwa (1659) that put Shuja, the second brother, out of reckoning. Aurangzeb designated Shubhkaran *subehdar* of Bundelkhand, an honour strongly resented by Champat Rai of Panna.

Shubhkaran thrived in battle, accompanying the Mughal forces to Balkh and Badakshan beyond the Hindu Kush and the Arakan on the empire's eastern frontier to fight the Burmese pirates. He led a large contingent to Bijapur and

◀ *The entrance to the Datia fortress-palace*

▶ *The uniformity and symmetry of Mughal-style architecture combined with Hindu motifs that typified the Datia style*

Purandar. Aurangzeb was aggrieved at the death of Shubhkaran. His son and successor was Dalpat Rao (1683–1707) who attained distinction in the Mughal campaigns against the Marathas.

Dalpat Rao was generously accorded courtesies in the Mughal court. The cordiality between the two extended to their spouses. Once, when Aurangzeb's begum was journeying from Burhanpur to Agra, she was escorted by Dalpat Rao and his Rani. Suddenly, the Rani's elephant became erratic when crossing the Sindh. There was apprehension about the Rani's *purdah* falling and her getting exposed. The Mughal begum unhesitatingly threw her *chadar* to the Rani, thus ensuring that the latter's honour was not compromised.

Dalpat Rao fought on the Mughal side against Bijapur, Golconda, Adoni and Gingee. From Gingee, he brought back a huge gate as a trophy, which was installed in Datia. Dalpat Rao was a perpetual campaigner, and during one of his long absences, a son usurped power. Aurangzeb's intervention enabled Dalpat Rao to regain his position when he returned. The emperor also allowed the Bundela chief to have an *alam*, or royal standard, before him.

Dalpat Rao died of wounds received in Jajau, the most important engagement in the Mughal civil war (1707) that followed Aurangzeb's death. In Datia, too, there was a battle among half-brothers regarding succession. Ultimately Ramchandra (1711–36) came to the throne. He fought on the side of Chhatrasal's son, Jagat Raj of Jaitpur, against Bangash Khan, Mughal governor of Farrukhabad. Later, Ramchandra went to aid the Nawab of Oudh against rebellious landlords, and was killed in battle.

With the Mughals in the grip of the Marathas, Datia came under pressure. But this did not dampen the imperial trappings. The emperor, Shah Alam, toured Bundelkhand in the monsoon of 1760 and received the then Datia chief, Indrajit (1736–62), at Banda, presenting him royal standards, musical instruments and a portable throne. The decline of the Peshwa following the third battle of Panipat in 1761 saw the Scindia's rise. The Datia chief, Shatrujit Singh (1763–1801), was killed in battle against the Scindia's troops — led by the Frenchman, Perron — at Seondha, on the banks of the Sindh.

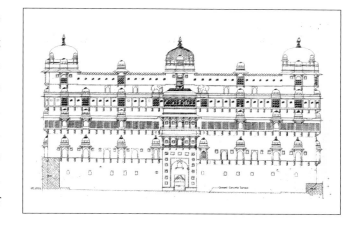

Datia under Parichhat (1801–39) — compelled by the freebooting Pindaris and Jhansi's Marathas — signed a treaty of alliance with the British in 1804. The resultant peace enabled Parichhat to sort out his domestic problems emanating from the numerous family trees from multiple marriages. The chief built a city wall with four massive gates. The next ruler, Vijay Bahadur (1839–57), led a *kirtan*-chanting religious life. He was followed by a minor, Bhawani Singh (1857–1907). Datia's Regent Rani saw the events of 1857 as a chance to cut Jhansi's Marathas to size.

Residential rooms at the Datia palace (inset) detail of the ornate carved ceilings

The Datia forces encircled Jhansi and waited six months for General Hugh Rose to launch his offensive. After the British took Jhansi, Moropant Tambe —the Rani of Jhansi's father — was captured in Datia while making a getaway, and handed over to the British. In 1865, the British approved the title of 'Maharaja' for Datia's ruler.

Pax Britannica saw the princes getting preoccupied with rankings and seating orders. Datia's Bhawani Singh attended the Viceroy's Durbar at Agra in 1866. According to an official account of the British:

'The gratifications afforded to the Treaty Chiefs of Bundelkhand, Datia, Orchha and Samthar was somewhat marred by a feeling of mortification at the position assigned them with reference to some of the Princes of Rajpootana of modern creation. The subject has been under report to the Government of India, but no definite decision has yet been given as to the exact position they are to occupy at future similar Durbars; the conflicting claims and pretensions of the several chiefs conceived, doubtless, making the settlement of this point a delicate and difficult matter .' (*Archive Collections*)

On his way to Datia, the French traveller Louis Rousselet had occasion to witness the Agra Durbar — 'a magnificent *coup-d'oeil* (1983, p 288)' — presided by the Viceroy, Sir John Lawrence (1863–69). It was a balmy November, when Rousselet saw '…a long procession of Boundelas and Rajpoot princes, all in rich and picturesque costumes: the Maharajah of Ourtcha, the Rao Maharajah of Duttiah, the Rajah of Sumpter, the Rajah of Chircari… (1983, pp 289-90)' Some weeks later, Rousselet was in Datia, standing before Bir Singh's fortress-palace:

'Everything about this palace is sombre and massive; and one can easily discern the traces of the great genius of King Bir Sing Deo, and of the notorious Boundela, whose name has become legendary. Its enormous proportions render it unfit for habitation; the small Court of Duttiah, indeed, would be lost in this immense labyrinth; and thus it is abandoned to the bats and the owls .' (1983, p 337)

Travellers from Agra to Jhansi see Bir Singh's fortress-palace at Datia looming over the surroundings, seemingly taller than its 130 feet. It looks southwards over a large lake, the Karan Sagar, constructed by Shubhkaran, who also built the palatial Rajgarh, used later for housing government offices. Bir Singh's edifice, which took nine years to complete, is in the form of a square, and built in stone and bricks without wood or iron. Wide eaves, lattices and overhanging balconies delineate its five storeys, each of different height.

The interior comprises a series of apartments with terraces, complemented by courtyards. The complex of chambers and corridors, pillars and arches, integrate well, manipulated to keep in perspective the panoramic views all around. The splendour of the complex is enhanced by arcades and kiosks, ribbed domes, and octagonal towers at the corners. Elaborate brackets support the balconies and oriel windows. The main dome, massive and secure, sits in the centre, guarded by large rooftop cupolas.

The Datia fortress-palace wears a shroud of silence. It had already been long deserted when visited by Governor -General Lord Hastings (1812–23) in 1818. Captain Sleeman saw the building in 1835 and was reflective on finding it abandoned; his hosts responded (1915, p 232):

'No prince these degenerate days could muster a family and court worthy of such a palace — the family and court of the largest of them would, within the walls of such a building, feel as if they were in a desert. Such palaces were made for princes of the older times, who were quite different beings from those of the present day.'

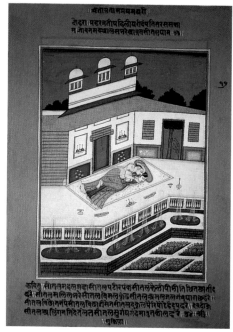

The Datia School of Art focused on the lifestyle of the elite classes (eighteenth century)

Samthar

Samthar fort arrived on the political landscape in a time of flux. The Maratha trajectory was on the rise and the British were getting into contention in central India. The Mughals were clearly fading out. An eighteenth century fort, it is believed that one of Babar's (1526–30) commanders, Shamsher, had built a *garhi*, a small fort, here, in the nature of an outpost. The site was referred to as Shamshergarh. The terrain was samtal— level; hence the name Samthar.

The rulers of Samthar were Bar-gujars, among the thirty-six Indian royal lines recognised by James Tod. The Bar-gujars were a section of the Gujars believed to have come to India with the white Hun hordes at the end of the fifth century. They attained laurels when they fought on the side of Prithviraj Chauhan against Muhammad Ghori (1191–92).

Samthar was part of the Datia kingdom. When the Datia ruler Ramchandra was killed in battle, there were many claimants to the throne. Naune Shah, a powerful zamindar, intervened, enabling the late king's great grandson Indrajit to ascend the throne. In reward, Naune Shah was awarded a *jagir* of five villages and the title of 'Rajdhar'; his son, Madan Singh, was assigned the governorship of Samthar fort. Madan Singh was succeeded by a son, Bishan Singh, who died childless.

A brother, Devi Singh (1780–1800), took over. Taking advantage of Datia's declining status, he began to govern as though Samthar were a separate kingdom. Samthar fort provided a base to Devi Singh for expanding his possessions. At the same time, he helped Datia tide over its adversities, emanating mostly from an overbearing Scindia in Gwalior and the Marathas in Jhansi.

In 1785, Samthar broke away. This political initiative was taken after taking the Peshwa into confidence. The Marathas were now dominant in Bundelkhand and it was only shrewd to have reached an accord with the Peshwa. Subsequently, the Peshwa bestowed the formal title of Raja on the Samthar chief, Ranjit Singh (1800–15).

The British also had to be convinced of Samthar's standing. The Samthar darbar approached the East India Company through the following statement:

'Our family is descended from the Bar-Gujar clan, one Suraj-Bans being the founder. His descendants were the rulers of Panchala, Sindh, Gujarat, etc. One Deo-sut held Gujarat and Mewat. Seventh in descent from him came Ked Rae, a very powerful chief, who held Gujarat when Alexander the Great invaded his dominions. Deo-sut came to terms with the Macedonian King and a great battle was thus avoided. This statement will be found to be fully borne out by the records of

▶ *Raj Mandir, Samthar*

Alexander's travels. Ked Rae's descendants ruled at Lahore for nine generations, the last king being Chandra Sen, who fought with and defeated Subuktagin, driving him back to Ghazni…'(Luard, 1907, p 28)

Ranjit Singh II (1815–27) entered into a treaty in 1817 with the East India Company on lines similar to that of Orchha and Datia. All three were designated 'treaty states'. These were states recognised by the British as possessing due autonomy and powers when the engagements of alliance were concluded. The other princely states in Bundelkhand were 'sanad states', like Charkhari or Ajaigarh, which pledged fidelity to the British and, in response, were confirmed in possession of their lands by the British through a grant. Overall, the British and the princely states bound themselves to assist each other in the hour of need.

Later, when Lakshmi Bai of Jhansi led the revolutionaries in central India, and the regent ranis of Orchha and Datia aided the British, Samthar also came to be guided by a rani, standing in for her incapacitated husband, Hindupat (1827–64). Samthar's regent power, Rani Lallan Ju, was pragmatic: she gave refuge to a number of British in her fort during the turbulence, and is believed by many to have also provided Rani Lakshmi Bai with a change of horses at a village, Datavali, when she was on her way from Jhansi to Kalpi in order to join Nana Sahib.

Hindupat had been retired to a *garhi* on the outskirts of the state, accompanied by his Muslim mistress and a son by her, Arjun Singh, also named Ali Bahadur. The contenders for succession were Ali Bahadur and Chhatr Singh, Hindupat's son from Rani Lallan Ju. The succession dispute was referred to the British who confirmed Chhatr Singh (1864–96) as the rightful heir to the throne.

From Samthar fort, drought, pestilence and relief works, land records, and justice were administered. Chhatr Singh, a progressive ruler, increased revenue and negotiated successfully with the British for the introduction of railways and irrigation canals. Samthar was afflicted with famine

◄ *Italianate facade of the seven-storey living quarters*

▲ *Entrance to the private residential quarters*

during the rule of Bir Singh Dev (1896–1935), which kept the state machinery occupied with various welfare activities. Radha Charan Singh was the last ruler (1935–49): he continued to reside in the fort after the merger of the princely states with the Union.

The fort battlements and crenellations behind a moat are well preserved. The elephant gates are awe-inspiring. Occasionally ornate, the residential part of the fort has long corridors and steep staircases leading to the rooms and courtyards. The living quarters in the fort comprise seven lofty storeys, easily the most imposing structure for hundreds of square miles around. The sense of permanence and tranquillity motivated the construction of elaborate living quarters, administrative buildings, record-rooms and courthouses.

The Samthar ruler was awarded the title of 'His Highness' and a salute of eleven guns during Delhi's Imperial Durbar of 1877. Samthar became typical of the leisured aristocracy of the days: European styles were in vogue; modern conveniences and toilets were introduced; there was *shikar* on every conceivable occasion. Ladies enjoyed bicycling which was done in *purdah* —

▲ *The moat surrounding Samthar fort*

huge curtains were stretched over distances. A menagerie of animals was also maintained in the Samthar fort, along with elephant houses. For the nobility, life was easy, lavish and elaborate.

As the foremost agriculturist in the area, the ruler would spend time supervising the sinking of wells and installation of irrigation devices. Milch animal breeding was promoted. Besides, there was benevolent patronage of temples, schools and hospitals.

Dussehra was an occasion for aplomb. The Maharaja would ride in an elephant procession with spearmen and lancers, fireworks and carriages. The wrestling pit came alive. Court routine comprised of *durbars*, with wizened peasants petitioning the ruler on his *masnad*, and the occasional full-throated poet reciting exaggerated paeans of praise. The picture was complete with chandeliers and *jagirdars*; assemblages in the courtyard passing cardamoms and sweatmeats around; dance performances and *qawwalis*, with the accompaniments of sarod, sarangi and pakhawaj.

A characteristic of princely life was the acquisition of badges of British favour. The criterion was unalloyed allegiance, with 1857 as the great watershed. Bir Singh Dev received the title of 'Maharaja' in 1898, as had his father Chhatr Singh in 1877. By now, the military had given way to a civilian rhythm, with red-tape in the government secretariat at Writers Building, Calcutta, knotting up all manner of questions, whether related to the cession of land for the Great Indian Peninsula Railway, salt levies, or the privilege to be addressed as a Maharaja.

Charkhari

Charkhari fort spreads over a rocky hill. The ramparts command a view of miles of wheat fields punctuated with mustard. The hill gradually descends into a sleepy town with tree-lined roads and horse *tongas* outracing bullock carts. The approach to the fort curves around the Ratan Sagar Lake, dotted with migratory birds.

The Raja of Jaitpur, Jagat Raj (1732–58) — a son of Chhatrasal — came to Charkhari to hunt a species of deer known as charkhar. On an auspicious *mangalwar* — Tuesday — in the dense forests of Ranjit hill, the raja laid the foundation of a fort: Mangalgarh. The raja's aim was to subdue the local Lodh community. A struggle ended in a compromise, with Jaitpur recognising the Lodh chieftain's *locus standi* with the awarding of a title. The ensuing peace paved the way for a new principality, Charkhari, to be carved out of an extended Jaitpur.

▲ *Ramparts of the Charkhari fort overlooking the Ratan Sagar lake*

Jagat Raj was succeeded at Jaitpur by his son, Pahar Singh. Tension arose because another son, Kirat Singh, had been nominated earlier as heir, but predeceased Jagat Raj. Kirat Singh's son, Guman Singh, tried to seize Jaitpur, and was checked by Pahar Singh. Guman Singh took refuge in Charkhari fort with his brother Khuman Singh. Reconciliation followed. Guman was settled in Ajaigarh-Banda and Khuman in Charkhari. Guman Singh died in 1781, leaving behind a minor son under the tutelage of his commander Arjun Singh.

Khuman Singh (1765–82) was the first Raja of Charkhari. He strengthened the fort parapets and sightings for musketry, and set up sturdy gates in the ascent. When the Oudh armies attacked Charkhari in 1768, Khuman Singh drove them off. Headstrong, Khuman Singh got needlessly provoked into battle by Arjun Singh and was killed in 1782.

Khuman Singh's son and successor was Vijay Bahadur (1782–1829). He approached the Scindia because his son had been kidnapped and held hostage in Gwalior by the Maratha tax collectors. The raja got his son back, but with Arjun Singh at his aggressive worst, Vijay Bahadur abandoned Charkhari to immerse himself in *pravachanas* and writings in the relative tranquillity of Jhansi. Charkhari became an annexe of Ajaigarh-Banda.

Vijay Bahadur broke out of his isolation, reaching out to Ali Bahadur, a favourite of the Peshwa, and Himmat Bahadur, a soldier-of-fortune, for help against Arjun Singh. Himmat Bahadur killed Arjun Singh in battle in 1791. Ali Bahadur usurped the throne to become the 'Nawab of Banda' and restored to Vijay Bahadur some territory with Charkhari fort. Vijay Bahadur was succeeded by a fourteen-year-old grandson

◄ *A reservoir with a Kali temple*

Ratan Singh (1829–60), from an illegitimate son.

Charkhari was the first state in Bundelkhand to seek British protection through a *sanad* and assure fealty (1804). During the 1857 uprising, Ratan Singh rushed a cannon and 200 matchlockmen to the neighbouring British district of Hamirpur. The Deputy Commissioner, T.K. Lloyd, and his deputy, Donald Grant, fled. They hid in some castor oil fields, but were

Entrance to the old palace, leading to the Charkhari fort. (Inset) Elephant spikes

detected, bound up and shot in the civil court compound. An anxious British magistrate from Mahoba, J.H.Carne, somehow reached Charkhari fort — to a hospitable reception. A furious Nana Sahib ordered Tatya Tope to undertake an all-out offensive against Charkhari. Tatya Tope's assessment, conveyed to Nana Sahib, was:

'It is very difficult to capture this fort, inasmuch as the place is hilly and I have only a small body of men with me. The Rajah does not wish to side with us, as he relies very much on the strength of the English. When such is the case, whatever services may be achieved by me will of course have its origin in your good fortune. The sepoys boast very much now but in the time of difficulty they will desert us. God does whatever is good. In the battle fought day

▲ *An arch decorated with floral designs in bright Bundela colours*

before yesterday, our troops fled before the enemy. I hope therefore that you will be pleased to send Vilayetee men [Afghans] to our assistance and one hundred pieces of cloth which I will distribute among the troops here as an inducement to them to take the field.'

(*Freedom Struggle in Uttar Pradesh*, 1959, pp 228-9)

When Tatya Tope received intelligence that the northwest portion of the Charkhari fort was weak and vulnerable to assault, a strong cannonade was launched at this point. The Nawab of Banda also sent a force to assist Tatya Tope. The Raja of Charkhari sued for peace. The rebels demanded three lakh rupees, the surrender of the Mahoba magistrate, Carne, and a visit by the Raja to Tatya Tope's camp with an assurance that he would join the revolutionaries.

The Raja insisted that there were no British officers in his fort. He also regretted his inability to come to Tatya Tope's camp because of an inconvenient swelling on his posterior. Tatya continued heavy firing on the fort and ordered that the town be pillaged. Large-scale arson followed, including in the Raja's palace, outside the fort. According to Carne :

'The Rajah's own residence has also been rifled of every particle of property which could be carried away, while costly mirrors, chandeliers, carpets, and other valuable fittings and furniture of English fashion were smashed to pieces and otherwise destroyed by the rebel mob. Elephants and horses with their trappings, carriages of various kinds, palanquins and other conveyances, camels and draught bullocks, all the cattle belonging to the inhabitants...have all fallen into the hands of the enemy.' (*Freedom Struggle in Uttar Pradesh*, 1959, p 241)

After eleven days of hard fighting, the town came into the hands of Tatya Tope along with twenty-four guns. Most of the population fled. Among those resisting, the role of women was notable. With kitchen utensils and grinding *moosal* stones, they killed a number of Tatya's men. At the same time, the Raja of Charkhari kept the negotiations open.

The Raja sent his young son with trusted counsellors to Tatya Tope along with a large sum of money. Meanwhile, Carne, the British magistrate sought by Tatya Tope, was smuggled out through the rebel barricade to Panna in the guise of a Bundela Rajput. The British were closing in. Tatya Tope also had to abandon operations when Nana Sahib ordered him to go to the aid of the Rani of Jhansi. Ratan Singh's Charkhari survived the odds.

Jaitpur, from where Charkhari had been carved in the eighteenth century, was annexed by the British in 1849 under Lord Dalhousie's Doctrine of Lapse. The Raja of Jaitpur, Parichhat Singh — openly inimical to the British — was deposed due to his role in the Bundela Rising of 1842. In 1857, his widowed queen raised the banner of revolt. A spirited woman, she took control of Jaitpur, but it was a short-lived triumph.

The British rewarded the Raja of Charkhari with a *khillat* — a sword of honour, land grant in perpetuity, the privilege of adoption and an eleven-gun hereditary salute. The gratification paid under coercion to the revolutionaries was returned to the raja. The Nawab of Banda, who helped Tatya Tope in Charkhari, was exiled and his property confiscated.

The state buildings that came up in Charkhari during the ensuing peace, incorporated European designs, Venetian-style blinds and Corinthian columns. The ruler was titled 'Maharajadhiraj Sipahdar-ul-Mulk'. Today, the old draperies are ready to fall to pieces at a touch. But the elephant spikes on the main gateway, leading from the town to the fort atop the hill, remain sharp and glistening as ever.

Talbehat

T he fort of Talbehat is on an elevation commanding a lake. *Tal* means 'lake' and *bihat,* 'village' in the language of the Gonds, earlier chieftains of this tract. The Gonds were hardy agriculturists: their water-embankments are still in use.

In the eighth century, power shifted from the Gonds to the Pratihara Rajputs and then, during the ninth century, to the Chandellas. Talbehat became a prominent settlement, a fact testified by the three Chandella temples in the fort's vicinity, one dedicated to Mahadeva and two to Vishnu. With the decline of the Chandellas, the Gonds reinstated their hold in the area.

Later, Talbehat became a Bundela stronghold. Jehangir's ascent in Delhi marked the replacement of Ram Shah at Orchha by his brother and the emperor's favourite, Bir Singh. Ram Shah was assigned a prosperous *jagir* (1608-12), where he laid the foundation of Talbehat fort.

The site of the fort was Narsinghpuri, referred to as such because of the temple of Narsingh, which came to be included within the fort precincts. Ram Shah's grandson Bharat Shah (1612–30) completed the fort in 1618. He helped the Mughals crush a revolt by Godarai, the *kiledar* of Chanderi fort. In turn, the emperor attached Chanderi to Bharat Shah's possessions.

Devi Singh (1630–63), son of Bharat Shah, was resolute in strengthening ties with the Mughals and was able to acquire substantial revenue-yielding lands. His interests were helped by the rebellion of Orchha's Jujhar Singh against the Mughals. Shahjehan needed an ally to restore his writ in Bundelkhand. With Jujhar Singh on the run and the Mughals in pursuit, Devi Singh was given the additional responsibility (1634–36) of administering Orchha.

Simultaneously, Devi Singh refurbished Talbehat fort. He strengthened the roughly hewn stone wall with earthwork and scarps. The main fortifications, from north to south, quite intact till today, comprise a mile-long thick wall on a low hill overlooking the town. Some frescoes survive close to the Narsingh temple.

The principal defence on the north was provided by a large lake of about 500 acres, which continues to irrigate the cultivation nearby. According to legend, a severe drought had occurred in the area. Brahmins fasted and did penance, followed by a human sacrifice. This culminated in water sprouting from the earth, resulting in this lake. Alongside, towards the south of the fort, is a Chandella embankment of large stone blocks and a dense wooded area.

▲ *The main gateway of the fort. (Inset) Wall fresco*

Talbehat was a quiet place. An incident is recalled even today, indicative of Mor Prahlad's debauched chiefdom (1802–42), a period tied up in Bundela-Maratha political jostling. Some young women, collecting foliage for an *akhshaya tritiya* ritual, took their lives after being kidnapped and ravished by the king's men in Talbehat fort. This is still remembered as a shattering violation of the spirit behind a long-standing local custom, obliging men to venerate women and demonstrate it by touching their feet, regardless of caste or class.

Since the shocking incident, the celebrations accompanying the ritual have never been held in Talbehat.

The power vacuum, fuelled by the Mughal collapse, prompted Gwalior's Scindia

◄ *Shiva temple, Talbehat –*
the sahasralinga bears a thousand
miniature lingas

to take an all-out offensive against the dissolute Mor Prahlad, who held Talbehat fort by virtue of his being the Raja of Chanderi-Banpur. Scindia's French commander, Colonel Jean-Baptiste, was supported by forty cannons. The vulnerable points in the defence were betrayed, enabling Baptiste to force an entry (1811). The defenders escaped by the lake, but the Scindia lost hundreds of men. Besides Talbehat, the Gwalior forces also occupied large areas in Chanderi and Banpur.

Talbehat fort, after its occupation by Scindia's forces, was besieged by Mor Prahlad's son, Mardan Singh. Baptiste was rushed by Scindia for relief to the defenders. Negotiations followed, prodded by the British — keen on good relations with the Bundelas to counter the Marathas. Some territory under Scindia's occupation, including Banpur, was restored to Mor Prahlad. In return, Mardan Singh lifted the siege on Talbehat.

In 1857, Talbehat became a rallying point for the rebel cause, with the Raja of Banpur, Mardan Singh (1842–58), proclaiming his support for the Rani of Jhansi. The revolutionaries overpowered the small garrison in the fort. The raja took up residence here and was adequately supplied with provisions and men from Banpur. He put up stubborn resistance against the British. According to a contemporary British Intelligence Report (*Freedom Struggle in Uttar Pradesh*, 1959, p 250):

'The Bazaar of Lullutpore has been plundered. The Chief of Baunpore is reported to have secured all the corn within his Ellaka and to have removed it to Tall Baihut and Chundeyree...The Chief collected all his Thakoors and told them that he was their well-wisher. If they wished to deliver him to the British authorities he was ready to meet their wishes. All the Thakoors took oaths to side with him and expressed their readiness to fight to the last.'

The fort fell to Hugh Rose in March 1858 and was plundered by the Madras Regiment and the Orchha troops. Since then, the fort has been in disuse, its crenellations curling silently over the flat-roofed brown and white houses of sleepy Talbehat town.

▶ *Steps leading down to the tal*

Barwasagar

The tumult of 1857–58 saw Hugh Rose emerge as the man-of-the-hour for the British campaign in central India. With his eighteen-pounders and eight-inch mortars, Rose won a decisive victory at Barwasagar against Tatya Tope, who was leading a force of 20,000 that was intended to reinforce Lakshmi Bai in Jhansi. This was a major setback for the Rani, as Barwasagar, close to the river Betwa, provided a strategic forward line for engaging the British.

Built early in the eighteenth century by Orchha's Udot Singh, the fort commanded an extensive view from the Betwa to Orchha — a skirmish-prone area, coveted both by the Marathas in Jhansi and Gwalior's Scindia. One such affray had been in 1744, when a brother of the Scindia was killed by the Orchha Bundelas.

Rani Lakshmi Bai's 1857–58 campaign saw her father Moropant Tambe take the initiative of capturing Barwasagar fort from the Orchha troops. He was aggressive; according to an abstract of the British Intelligence:

'The Ranee of Jhansee's troops that are stationed at Burwa Saugor plundered the…villages…They cut down the flag staff at Niwaree, pulled down the government buildings and burnt the village. All the supplies collected for the British camp have been taken by them.

The cattle in the village…have been lifted…Mama Sahib the Ranee's father are all … stationed at Burwa Saugor.' (*Freedom Struggle in Uttar Pradesh*, 1959, p 288)

After Tatya Tope's rout by the British, the Rani's troops retreated from Barwasagar to Jhansi.

Post-mutiny, a new order arrived. Louis Rousselet, a Frenchman, visited Barwasagar in 1867. By now, the fort had been converted into a resthouse for touring officers, surveyors and sundry picnickers. Rousselet wrote :

'Barwa-Sagur…The castle stands upon the side of a hill…having nothing Hindoo about it…with its large round towers and its many-windowed facades, it would not be out of place upon the hills that surround the Rhine…'(1983, p 346)

Visitors were careful not to stray too far. Rousselet recalled how one of his camels, negligently let loose at night, was killed by a tiger on the prowl. He mentions crocodiles in the adjacent lake

▲ *The fort overlooking Barwasagar lake, used for irrigation*

— which was formed when Raja Udot Singh erected an embankment across a feeder stream of the Betwa. A looping flight of steps descending into the water presents a pleasing sight from atop the fort.

When the Raj rose from the ashes of John Company, the ruling class acquired a new ruddiness and self-assurance. The discipline associated with district administration was framed in manuals and regulations. Field inspections and partals were central to governance, necessitating 'night-halts', for which the facilities at Barwasagar were convenient. The basic nature of the amenities was amply compensated by the chef creating his culinary wonders on the mud oven.

Rousselet recorded his experience in the fort:

'Having lighted torches, we began by visiting the apartments of the castle. The ground floor consists of large vaulted rooms, the large windows of which look out upon a deep precipice near the lake; and a winding staircase leads to the first floor…Upon the second floor…some smaller and more comfortable apartments…These rooms at the top of the palace are partly surrounded by a terrace overlooking the lake…Our camp was soon installed in its aerial

abode, and a good dinner obliterated the recollection of our inconveniences during the day…' (1983, p 345)

From the time Victoria was declared Empress of India in 1877 to the outbreak of the Second World War, life in the districts remained the same: meals by lamplight, the hand-pulled fan in the summers, mosquito nets, comfortable armchairs, gymkhanas and bath houses, topees and sola hats, felt and canvas *shikari* helmets, turbans and cummerbunds, chefs and retainers, water carriers, *dhobis*, and *mussalchees* — all completed the picture.

◄ *An alcove in the fort*

▲ *Residential section of the fort*
▶ *(Inset) Surviving graffitti on the walls by British occupants during the Raj*

The Raj had its heroes, and pomp and ceremony were encouraged to emphasise the existence of imperial power. But much more striking was the day-to-day exercise of governance kept ticking by the ordinary field officers, civil and military. Sport was an essential ingredient: riding, pig-sticking and hunting wild boar were popular pastimes. In the shrubbery of Barwasagar lake, there was a surfeit of partridge. Wild geese were aplenty. The lake teemed with fowl, wilder than the quilt of lilies and lotuses.

The fort is crumbling, but the air of timelessness and languor is inescapable. Moth-eaten records tell the story of a bygone era — of self-righteousness and arrogance. And, of officers who stood in the fort resthouse at sunset, looking on to the countryside drenched in orange after a hectic day of village inspections and snipe shooting.

Nothing has changed. Nearby is a Chandella irrigation dam. Fishermen cast their nets from canoes hollowed out of tree trunks. During the winter crop, the landscape is a mosaic of green-brown cultivation, interspersed with honey gold. The odd visitor is seen, come to view the fort in the crimson pall of an evening and experience the gay abandon of Bundela folk songs.

Deogarh

The Betwa washes past Deogarh, a treasure house of sculptures secured within craggy rock formations. Set on a tableland at the end of a range of low hills, the history of the fort encompasses epochs from the Guptas to the Bundelas.

The flow of its tale is as smooth as the dancing lines in the carved doorway of Deogarh's temple of the Gupta period, a fantasy in stone, dating back fifteen centuries. It is as calm as nature's blue and green, so bountiful in this *garh* of the *devtas*.

The Betwa and the sheer rock face alongside provide a natural defence to the fort. Located on the right bank of the river, the fortifications extend over a vast area, 300 feet above the plains, with overhanging cliffs forming a steep sandstone ridge. A thriving civic community, adroit in trading and skilled in the arts, lived here. Deogarh provided protection and plenty of opportunities to prosper and engage in cultural and religious pursuits.

The Deogarh fort was built by the Kannauj Pratiharas in the ninth century to ward off the Rashtrakuta challenge from the Deccan. Nagabhata (800–825), king of Kannauj, had suffered reverses in battle near Jhansi at the hands of the Rashtrakuta, Govind III (808–814). The need was felt to secure the Betwa as a line of defence. Deogarh provided an ideal site. An inscription dated Samvat 919 (AD 862) in the fort indicates the importance accorded to Deogarh by the great Pratihara king, Bhojdeva of Kannauj (836–885).

Another inscription of Samvat 1154 (AD 1097) on the southwestern edge of the hill at Raj Ghati refers to the fort-complex as Kirtigiri, named after the Chandella king Kirtivarman (1060–1100). The Chandellas captured the fort from the Kalachuris of Chedi. Chandella credence and self-assurance was in evidence. The dynasty was peaking in various endeavours — reflected in Krishna Misra's Sanskrit allegorical drama *Prabodha-chandrodaya*. Often enacted before Kirtivarman, it was a work based on Vedanta philosophy, with striking representations of knowledge and devotion.

A Chandella minister, Vatsaraj, strengthened the fort, conscious of the earlier expeditions of Mahmud of Ghazni to Bundelkhand. Deogarh also became the base for Chandella activities against Dhar's Paramaras.

Centuries later, the Bundelas carried out major repairs to the fort. Deogarh was now part of the Chanderi fiefdom assigned by Jehangir to Ram Shah after his younger brother Bir Singh was given Orchha. The Bundelas held Deogarh till the Scindia took it in 1811 during his Chanderi campaign handled by Colonel Jean-Baptiste. The Frenchman was rewarded with

▶ *A path cut into a cliff face overlooking the Betwa at Deogarh*

a *jagir* at Jariya near Deogarh, where his descendants still live.

The innermost citadel of Deogarh's fortifications is approached through two gates. Within the precincts, there are some thirty temples, with images inset haphazardly on the walls of courtyards or lined along pathways. Sculptural pieces lie scattered. The silence is absolute as the visitor ploughs through the undergrowth into the *ghati* below on the Betwa. There was a time when, across the river, tigers roamed free.

The remains of a shrine are seen in the southwest corner of the fort. Built on a high plinth, it was dedicated to Varaha, the third incarnation of Vishnu. Amidst the ruins is a sixth century life-size image of Nrivaraha — man and boar combined — gleaming in a trickle of moonlight. The absence of a superstructure makes it difficult to determine the temple's design, but it appears to have been redone a couple of times. A number of panels dating back to the eighth century have been unearthed from this site.

Rock-cut caves are located at the river-gate in the south of the fort area. Here, the gods are in a state of spiritual equilibrium. Many of the rock formations appear strange — scoured as they are into forms resembling temple spires, runaway bulls and other shapes, a product both of natural weathering and manual carving. This is where the Betwa takes a sharp turn to the east. Along a cliff face, in the Nahar Ghati, are several niches and a bas-relief of the Saptmatrika, with a standing figure of Surya holding lotus flowers. Mahishasura-mardini occupies a spot in the Siddh-ki-gufa, depicting the goddess Durga killing a buffalo-headed *asura*, or demon.

Mahishasura- mardini

▲ *The Siddh-ki-gufa*

The sixth century Dasavatara temple is dedicated to Vishnu. The idol in the *garbagraha* is missing, but the panel carvings are there, which master craftsmen enlivened with mythological and metaphysical tales. The friezes depict scenes from the Ramayana, the Mahabharata, Krishna's life and Vishnu's *avataras*. Conspicuous is the high platform on which the temple stands, originally adorned by continuous rows of sculptured panels on all four sides. Today, only a couple of reliefs can be seen embedded, with many others kept in storage. It is remarkable for a place of worship dating back to the Guptas to have survived so long in Bundelkhand.

It was during the Gupta period that the general form of the Hindu temple was established. Until then, temples were either rock-cut or flat-roofed structures. By the fifth century, there emerged the Hindu temple as an architectural reconstruction of the home of the Gods. The concept of stupa mounds that clung to the earth also transformed into taller structures reaching skywards. The period marked a new phase in the styles of temple architecture —the *nagara* and the *dravida*, which developed into the *shikharas* of the north and the *vimanas* of the south. The Dasavatara temple is, however, not the most representative of the *nagara* temples, with their

▲ *Gajendra moksha panel at the Vishnu Dasavatara Temple, Deogarh*

cruciform plans and curvilinear *shikharas*. There has, however, been a clear effort at Deogarh to obtain a semblance of height by moving away from the conventional flat roof. Excavations reveal the existence of small square shrines at each corner, which, with the central russet-hued structure, constituted the earliest examples of the *panchayatana* type of temple architecture.

The classic beauty of the Dasavatara temple is enhanced by sculptured niches on three sides, each in the form of a sunken panel between pilasters, and on the fourth by an exquisitely carved doorway with *mithunas* (dancing figures), *pramathas* (dwarfish male figures) and *patravallari* (a variety of creepers). A *lalatabimba* (projecting image) in the centre of the upper lintel shows Vishnu on an *ananta* (cosmic serpent) with a canopy of seven hoods. The deity, uniquely, is flanked by two of its own incarnations, *Nrisimha* (man-lion) and *Vamana* (dwarf) — a feature unknown in Indian iconography. *Apsaras* hold aloft the pillars. The Gajendra-moksha panel on the north, noble in proportions, depicts Vishnu with four arms, freeing Gaja from the grip of the serpent Naga. The emancipator, accompanied by *gandharvas*, descends from heaven on the wings of Garuda. For all its massiveness, the movement appears weightless. Love and gratitude stream from Gaja as he makes a floral offering to the Omnipotent.

The Anantsayi Vishnu panel on the south face of the Dasavatara temple shows the Lord of the Universe in slumber on the coils of the seven-hooded Shesha-naga. Lakshmi sits at his feet.

Anantsayi Vishnu panel at the Dasavatara Temple depicting Vishnu reclining on the coils of the Shesha-naga. Chaturanan Brahm is seated on a lotus emerging from Vishnu's navel

▲ *The Nar Narayana panel is on the east wall of the Dasavatara Temple*

Soaring above are Kartikeya, Indra, Mahadeva and Parvati, airborne on their *vahanas*. Below are other richly embellished figures; earlier thought to represent the five Pandavas and Draupadi, these figures are now believed to be Madhu, Kaitabha and the four Ayudha-purushas.

The Nar Narayana panel is on the east wall of the Dasavatara temple. Flying *vidyadharas* carry a canopy of foliage above Narayana. This symbolises the fusion of the divine and the human: the lion and the deer are in amity; strength from asceticism overcomes all failings of the flesh. Peace is tangible in a composition of overwhelming simplicity and power.

Deogarh was a Jain centre of significance from the post-Gupta period up to the seventeenth century. There are, thus, hundreds of Jina images in Deogarh. Panels depict Jain mythology, including the penance of Bahubali, the birth of the *tirthankaras*, *acharyas* and *upadhyayas* in meditation and *ambikas* in ecstatic poses. Jain temple architecture includes the *manastambha* (votive pillar), *pratimasarvo-bhadrika* (Jina image visible from all sides) and *sahastrakuta* (pillar carved with a thousand Jina figures).

▶ *A Jain temple, Deogarh – the shikhara, in nagara style, is surmounted by a circular amalaka*

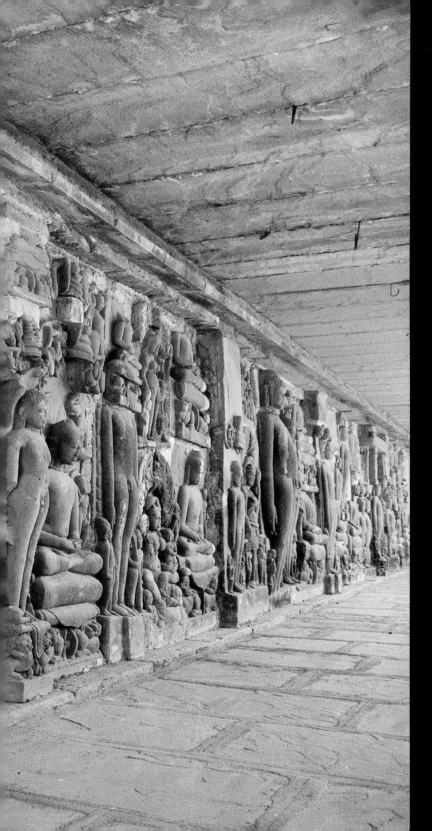

▲ *A manastambha (votive pillar) in the courtyard of the Jain complex. Deogarh was one of the places in Bundelkhand where Jainism flourished. The tradition to erect pillars before shrines dates back to the second century. The votive pillars were erected in an open area to enable assembly and obeisance from all four sides. Jains adopted prototypes of Hindu deities, for example Ambika corresponded to Durga.*

◄ *The twenty four Jain Tirthankaras – beginning with Adinath and ending with Mahavira – in varied mudras*

The Jain temples, enclosed within an inner surrounding wall, are in the eastern part of the fort. Spangling the sky is the Shantinath temple. Its graceful arcade comprises six rows of six pillars each, decked with a profusion of arabesques and geometrical patterns. This multi-pillared hall has a raised platform in the centre. Jain figures embellish the approach to the sanctum. Soft light filtering through an opening blurs the details of an ebony statue of Shantinath — the sixteenth *tirthankara* — with the *antarala* in front and surrounded by a *pradakshinapath*. The Shantinath temple was in existence when Bhojdeva came to power in Kannauj during the ninth century.

The workmen who created Deogarh still live. They fashioned the sublime to give poise and proportion to the gods, as well as painstakingly crafting the routine — door-lintels, decorated pillars and accessories. The treasures must not get lost. Deogarh has suffered, and not only because of wind and rain. The sharpness of many an image has become blurred. Missing reliefs testify to rampant vandalism. Amateurish repairs have taken a toll. Skills and surgery, including bracing and stone transplants, are needed. The chronicle must survive in Deogarh.

Door frame of the Jain Shantinath Temple, Deogarh
decorated with motifs of devis, devtas and dwarapalas

Dhamoni

The *Ain-i-Akbari* refers to Dhamoni as an administrative unit in Raisen, part of the Malwa province. Even before the Mughals, Dhamoni was an important trading mart of the Malwa kingdom and a market for elephants captured from the jungles nearby.

Thick vegetation surrounds Dhamoni, the last refuge of Orchha's Jujhar Singh who had rebelled against Shahjehan. This hostility was traced to when Shahjehan, still Prince Khurram, challenged the authority of his father, Jehangir. To discipline Khurram, the emperor turned to his confidante: Bir Singh, the then Orchha chief. The Bundela king responded by deputing a cavalry contingent under his son Jujhar Singh, a plucky horseman, but with a penchant for needless ruffling and hardly possessing the suavity required for such a delicate mission.

The equation between Orchha and the Mughals became insurmountably frosty when Jujhar Singh succeeded Bir Singh and Khurram took over as Shahjehan. The bitterness escalated when Jujhar Singh plundered the Gond fort of Chauragarh (1634) and killed its chief Prem Narayan. Bundela-Gond rivalry was long standing, but this particular act of aggression deliberately ignored

Shahjehan's express wishes that the Gonds be left alone. The Mughals resolved to punish Orchha.

Jujhar Singh took refuge in Dhamoni. He fled as the Mughals drew near, leaving behind a contingent at the fort with a commander, Ratnai. The Bundelas razed the houses and cleared the thickets around the fort to deny the enemy cover. Deep ditches were dug on the west of the fort, while natural precipices protected the southern and northeastern flanks. The defenders fought well, but stray shells ignited the gunpowder stored in the towers. In the ensuing panic, the besiegers carried the day by sheer numbers. The imperial forces recovered substantial treasure thrown into wells by the fleeing Bundelas.

It was a young Aurangzeb who led the Mughal campaign. The hostile terrain was brimming with Bundela irregulars, as the future emperor set out to trap Jujhar Singh who had taken flight with his family and *zenana*, southwards. There was a heavy Gond presence in this area and the Mughals did not have to exert themselves much. The Gonds caught up with the fleeing Bundelas. The outnumbered Bundelas killed many of their women and disfigured the others to remove the possibility of them being made members of a Mughal harem. The fugitives then turned around to fight. Jujhar Singh and his son were brutally slain and their heads were strung up at the gates of Sihora town.

Aurangzeb was happy to be able to rest awhile in Dhamoni fort. Originally, a modest fort — a *garhi* — it was built in the fifteenth century by a Gond chieftain, Surat Shah, of the Garhmandla dynasty. A resurgent Bir Singh of Orchha took the fort from the Gonds and decided to strengthen it. Astrologers were consulted and the fort, constructed in a roughly triangular shape, was rebuilt, utilising where possible, the earlier foundation material.

The main gateway, with its barbican, leads into a courtyard. This is followed by another entrance into the interior of the fort. Occupying an area of about fifty acres, the fort included residences and facilities for dispensing affairs of state, befitting the status of an administrative hub. Remnants of the Rani Mahal and *kutcherry* can still be seen. Bir Singh's son, Narhardas, held court in the fort and administered revenue collection from here.

After Aurangzeb took Dhamoni, a regular *kiledar*, Sardar Khan, was appointed. However, de facto control of the hinterland outside the immediate pale of the fort remained with the Bundelas; a fact with which the Mughals came to acquiesce. Dhamoni came under strain with the ascent of Panna under Champat Rai and his formidable son Chhatrasal.

Captain Sleeman

Dhamoni lay on the road to the trading city of Sironj, sixty-five miles west — a target for the Panna Bundelas. Khaliq, a Mughal *kiledar* of Dhamoni, posted *faujdars* on the trunk routes and horse-pickets to counter pillaging by Chhatrasal and his son Hirde Shah. Aurangzeb had hoped to make Dhamoni the launch pad for his Deccan campaign, but could not because of his inability to rein in the freebooters that spawned in the area.

Chhatrasal's campaign in and around Dhamoni lasted three decades till the end of the seventeenth century. Chhatrasal defeated the *kiledar* Khaliq, and successors, Rahullah Khan and Sadr-ud-din, in pitched battles. In 1680, Chhatrasal took Sadr-ud-din prisoner; he was released on payment of a huge ransom. Chhatrasal's war of attrition led to a rapid turnover of *kiledars* in Dhamoni fort. Chhatrasal killed Ikhlas Khan, a *kiledar*, in battle. In another engagement, the Bundela forces wounded a Mughal general Bahlol Khan, who succumbed in Dhamoni fort.

The Mughals were drained out and Chhatrasal was able to occupy the fort in 1700. Aurangzeb accepted the situation and awarded Chhatrasal the title of 'Raja'. His son Hirde Shah succeeded in 1731. The local land-owning Lodhs were appointed as keepers of the fort; they doubled up as revenue officials in the area. In 1799, the fort was ceded to the Maratha Bhonsles of Nagpur.

The British were not far behind. Major General Marshall's forces besieged the fort in 1818 — part of a mopping-up exercise after the conclusion of the Anglo-Maratha wars. The Bhonsles put up stiff resistance and the British had to mount an assault on Dhamoni fort. The attempt was successful. A British priority in these parts was the anti-Thugee campaign, which brought Captain Sleeman to Dhamoni in the 1830s.

Sleeman wrote about Dhamoni:

'The only thing remarkable here is the magnificent fortress, which is built upon a small projection of the Vindhya range, looking down on each side into two enormously deep glens...The rays of the sun seldom penetrate to the bottom of these glens, and things are, in consequence, grown there that could not be grown in parts more exposed...Bir Singh laid the foundation in the same happy hour which had been pointed out to him by his astrologers...The fortress is now entirely deserted, and the town, which the garrison supported, is occupied by only a small police-guard, stationed here to see that robbers do not take up their abode among the ruins.' (1915, pp 110-11)

Sleeman strengthened the token force already in the fort. Its ramparts, fifty feet high, and walls, fifteen feet thick, were clearly a vantage point for strengthening operations to eliminate banditry — a challenge in Bundelkhand. Some thirty years later, when the surveyor-traveller Louis Rousselet toured the area, the pall of banditry hung heavy; the Frenchman observed (1983, p 335): 'Bundelcund still continues to be the classic land of brigandism; and in its sombre forests was born the terrible religion of the Thugs'.

Dhamoni, in Mughal times, was the administrative centre of many hundreds of villages. It became a regional centre of learning, also maintaining close links with Akbar's religious experiments and orientation towards spirituality. Sheikh Faizi, poet and elder brother of Akbar's prime minister, Abul Fazl, was born here. The two brothers and their father, Sheikh Mubarak, an innovative religious teacher, prevailed upon Akbar to recite the *khutba* from the pulpit at Fatehpur Sikri — a step that provoked debate about the emperor's pretensions to spiritual authority.

Sheikh Faizi was Akbar's envoy to Khandesh and Ahmadnagar. His mentor, Baljati Shah, lived in Dhamoni; he was the inspiration behind the effusive *khutba* that Faizi had composed in verse. Baljati Shah's final resting place is near Dhamoni fort. For its upkeep, Aurangzeb declared two villages revenue-free. An *urs* is held here annually, the only time when a lost Dhamoni reverberates with human activity.

Chanderi

In 1528, Chanderi fort was a rallying point for the Rajputs against Babar, founder of the Mughal dynasty in India. Only a year earlier, Babar had decimated the Rajput confederacy — led by Maharana Sanga of Mewar — at Khanwah, near Agra. Now, under the command of Medini Rai, the Raja of Chanderi, the situation was waiting to erupt.

Medini Rai's contribution at Khanwah had included 12,000 handpicked horsemen, which matched his status as king-maker of Malwa. But Medini's strength was severely depleted. The raja was contemplative as he waited for Babar, surveying the silhouette of turrets and towers, minarets and domes, and the picturesque lakes stretching away from the fort over a wide countryside towards the surrounding tree-covered hillsides.

▲ *A Jauhar memorial at Chanderi*

The inns of Chanderi, a flourishing city, were humming with spies and Babar was aware of Medini Rai's worries. Keen to secure the route to the south, Babar proposed a settlement, which the Rajput chief rejected. As Babar approached, the bustling bazaars of Chanderi closed down and fell silent. Workmen weaving the fine muslin and gold thread Chanderi sarees fled. The siege lasted a month, till the Mughals located a vulnerable point in the defences to affect a breach. There were waves of warriors and an escalade. After beating back the Mughal army several times, the defenders donned saffron for the last encounter. They charged out with naked swords. With the men in close combat, the Rajput women, accompanied by children, committed *jauhar*.

Babar recorded in his autobiography, the *Babar-nama* :

'…the fort-walls, being entirely of stone, were extremely strong…the pagans…put many of our men to flight; they made them fly over the ramparts; some they cut down and killed…they put all their ladies and beauties to death, then, looking themselves to die, came naked out to fight…A pillar of pagan heads was ordered set up…' (2003, pp 595-6)

▼ *The Dilli Darwaza in Chanderi's outer fortifications*

◀ *The Khuni Darwaza from where prisoners were led to their deaths*

Situated on a sandstone hill, the Chanderi fort is 250 feet above the plains and the Kirat Sagar, which constituted an important source of water. The citadel's ramparts and towers convey the once great strength of the citadel. First fortified in the tenth century by the Chandellas, the stronghold extends for more than a mile north to south. The depth is three-fourths of a mile. There are a number of gateways. The entrance to the fort is through the Khuni Darwaza, or Bloody Gate, from where condemned prisoners were hurled to their deaths.

According to the notes of Captain J. Fenwick, a British army engineer, 150 years ago:

'The fort of Chandairee stands on an isolated hill in the midst of a hilly and jungly country, the natural defences of which are very great. These have been strengthened by a loopholed wall of about 10 feet in height, along which a number of tower bastions are placed at intervals. From a range of hills...a spur of land approaches to within 300 yards of one of the strongest of these towers and is connected with it by a natural causeway of solid rock through a ditch 30 feet in breadth and 12 in

▶ *Chanderi fort overlooking Kirat Sagar– the lake was an important source of water*

► *Kati Ghati, built by Chanderi's governor Sher Khan*

depth...The Tower Bastions, five in number, are very strongly built, fenced with cut stone and averaging 30 feet in diameter...the south-east corner defending the causeway has two towers one square the other circular with a short curtain between...is of great height and thickness...' (*Freedom Struggle in Uttar Pradesh*, 1959, pp 272-3)

Chanderi had been the seat of a powerful Hindu kingdom in the thirteenth century, extending over Bundelkhand and Malwa. The Delhi Sultan, Nasir-ud-din (1246–66), fielded a powerful army in 1251 under Balban to subdue Chanderi. The Chanderi Raja, Chahad Dev—a descendant of Prithviraj Chauhan of Delhi— whose dominions included Narwar, put 2,00,000 footmen and a cavalry of 5,000 in combat. But Balban prevailed, and Chanderi, along with Narwar, became part of the Sultanate.

The Delhi Sultanate's hold over Malwa and Chanderi weakened during the declining days of the Slave dynasty (1206–90). The Khilji dynasty (1290–1320) tevived Delhi's hold in 1305: the Sultan, Ala-ud-din (1296–1316), despatched a strong army under Multan's Governor, Ain-ul-Mulk — later, Malwa's *subehdar* — against Haranand, chief of Malwa and Chanderi, who fielded 1,00,000 men and 40,000 horses. The Sultanate's authority was restored.

▲ *Interiors of Kushak Mahal, originally a seven-storey palace*

Ala-ud-din's general Malik Kafur devastated the area around Chanderi (1309) en route to his Warangal campaign. He passed through Erich. Local residents recount Malik Kafur's four-day halt at Erich. Two centuries later, on his way to Chanderi, Babar also broke his journey at Erich for a day. Malwa's jurisdiction included Chanderi. Its fort became a recruitment centre for the Sultan's Deccan troops. The Moroccan traveller Ibn Batutah visited Chanderi in 1335 during the reign of Sultan Muhammad Tughlak (1325–51). In view of its importance, Chanderi was held by the Sultan's brother-in-law, Saif-ul-Mulk.

The anarchy following Timur's invasion led to Malwa's governor Dilawar Khan declaring his independence in 1401. He was a descendant of Muhammad Ghori, who had defeated the Delhi Chauhans to set up the Delhi Sultanate. Malwa's Ghoris folded up in 1436 after a Khilji minister, Mahmud, poisoned the king. The Khiljis ruled Malwa till 1531 when the kingdom was annexed by Gujarat.

Mahmud Khilji (1436–69) had to overcome Chanderi's Rajputs to make Malwa a powerful kingdom. Just a year before Mahmud's ascent, Chanderi had been seized by Maharana Kumbha of Mewar. The Rajputs had taken Kumbha's help in their revolt against Chanderi's governor. In 1438, Mahmud Khilji laid siege to Chanderi. The Mewar-backed garrison in the fort resisted for eight months. Mahmud had to direct the final assault himself to capture the fort. The Malwa ruler found Chanderi convenient for mobilising operations against the Jaunpur Sharqis on the northeastern border.

Mahmud left a mark at Chanderi with his architecture in the mid-fifteenth century. The Kushak Mahal, forty yards on each side, had seven storeys. Four survive. Its vibrant distinctiveness came from a set of lofty, arched passageways and quadrants and impressive interiors with their pierced screen-work, brackets and cornices. Balconied windows generously allowed natural lighting of the palace halls. The Badal Mahal Darwaza — erected by Mahmud at the base of the hill — was a commemorative gateway, an outlandish combination of arches and buttresses.

Chanderi's architecture, indicative of Malwa's all-embracing tradition, was exposed to Gujarat's influence, which can be seen in its arches, vaults and high quality masonry. Artisans were available from Ahmedabad — a city rich with craftsmen guilds open to opportunities for trading their skills. During the same period, the Jama Masjid of Chanderi came up, comprising an impressive frontage with bays and bold arches. The presence of Hindu masons is evident from the undulating brackets holding the eaves, a Hindu temple feature grafted onto a mosque. These buildings were precursors to the

▶ *Kushak Mahal*

architecture that evolved in Bundelkhand, blending Islamic and Hindu structural characteristics.

Mahmud's son and successor was the harem-centric Ghiyas-ud-din (1469–1500), controlled by Chanderi's governor, Sher Khan. When Delhi's Sultan Bahlol Lodi ventured close to Chanderi, he was met head-on and sent packing by Sher Khan. The governor is also credited for the Kati Ghati — an engineering innovation of considerable proportions — built in a cliff, southwest of the fort. This hillside cutting was used centuries later by Colonel Jean-Baptiste to transport guns for Daulat Rao Scindia's Chanderi operations and by Hugh Rose in the later stages of the 1857–58 campaign to regain the fort.

Ghiyas-ud-din Khilji was poisoned by a son, Nasir-ud-din. The resulting political uncertainty stoked Sher Khan's ambitions. He revolted, but was killed. The new king, Nasir-ud-din (1500–10), rode to Sher Khan's still fresh grave, exhumed his body, and perched it prominently on the walls of Chanderi fort. Nasir-ud-din was also poisoned like his father.

Medini Rai rose to power on account of his assistance to the Malwa king Mahmud Khilji II (1510–31), who was seeking to consolidate his kingship. Mahmud, driven out of his capital Mandu by adversary nobles, sought refuge in Chanderi fort. He was refused entry by Bihajat Khan, Chanderi's governor. The king appealed to Medini Rai, then chief of a small district. Medini, by ruse and force, got the gates of Chanderi fort opened. With reinforcements from Chanderi, Mahmud marched on Mandu and established himself. Medini Rai was made a minister and governor of Chanderi.

Not before long, Mahmud began to feel

◀ *A prayer hall at the Jama Masjid, Chanderi, built in the Malwa tradition*

▶ *Badal Mahal Darwaza – a triumphal archway erected by Mahmud Khilji*

THE FORTS OF BUNDELKHAND

▲ *Remnants of the inner citadel of Chanderi*

harried by the Rajputs. He tried to dismiss and even assassinate Medini, but failed. In desperation, Mahmud sought help from Gujarat. A countermove came from Maharana Sanga of Mewar, a willing ally of Chanderi against Mahmud. In the ensuing Medini–Mahmud battle (1520), 20,000 were killed, including Medini Rai's nineteen-year-old son. The victorious Rajputs took Mahmud prisoner, but released him later.

Medini Rai was described by Babar as 'a pagan of great consequence' (Smith, 2004, p 322). The Rajput was killed defending Chanderi (1528) against the Mughals. Events took a turn: in 1530 Babar died suddenly; a year later, a large part of Malwa was annexed by Gujarat and Chanderi was plundered. The Mughals were driven into exile by Sher Shah Sur, who became Delhi's Sultan (1540–45). Puran Mal of Raisen seized Chanderi fort amidst great slaughter. Sher Shah struck back ferociously, forcing Puran Mal's garrison at Chanderi to surrender. Puran Mal was captured and killed, three of his nephews castrated and a daughter made a dancing girl.

Chanderi remained part of the Malwa province when the Mughals returned from their exile (1540–55) in Persia. Chanderi was a prosperous commercial centre in Akbar's time, with a population of 3,00,000, and a large number of markets and caravan inns. Jehangir assigned Chanderi to the Talbehat chief, Bharat Shah, a Bundela from the house of Orchha — a reward for having subdued a rebellion by the *kiledar* of Chanderi fort.

Much of Maratha expansion in Bundelkhand during the eighteenth century was at Bundela expense. Chanderi's vulnerability was exposed when Malhar Rao Holkar of Indore invaded the area in 1735. Chanderi again appeared rudderless when its ruler Ramchandra (1775–1802), remorseful on having murdered a rival uncle, retired to Ayodhya for penance, leaving his state to an ineffective regent. The Scindia despatched Colonel Jean-Baptiste to Chanderi to pre-empt Sagar's Marathas from exploiting the power vacuum.

The Scindia occupied the forts at Chanderi, Talbehat and Banpur. Some thirty villages were

▼ *Chanderi's Ramnagar Mahal built by the Bundelas – late seventeenth century*

▲ *A weaver at his loom, weaving the famous Chanderi sari*
◄ *A typical Chanderi sari motif*

left for the sustenance of the Chanderi ruler, Mor Prahlad. The power imbalance moved the British to intercede. Banpur was returned to Mor Prahlad, which became his headquarters. Mor Prahlad's successor Mardan Singh sought Chanderi. An astute Scindia transferred the high revenue-yielding lands, including Chanderi and its fort, to the British.

Mardan Singh was disappointed, and in 1857 he became an ally of the Rani of Jhansi. The revolutionaries got possession of the fort when its garrison switched sides. The British recapture of Chanderi fort in 1858 is described in Captain Fenwick's account from the battlefront:

'…March 5 – The Brigade…took the strong line of masonry defences which extends across the valley by a *coup de main*, the enemy retreating in haste to the Fort…At night the Artillery brought up 28 inch mortars…Working parties were employed in throwing up a small breastwork in front of one of these mortars…Party…cutting road of approach through the jungle…Battery for two 8 inch mortars and one 8 inch howitzer with magazine commenced at sunset…Great difficulty experienced in coiling a place for the platform on account of the rocky nature of the ground…Subdued the enemy's fire…March 17 – The assault took place at 5 a.m. The enemy were surprised and the columns entering at the separate points…they retired precipitately from the Fort throwing themselves over the walls…'(*Freedom Struggle in Uttar Pradesh*, 1959, pp 273-5)

Chanderi fort appears heedless of its eventful past. Maharana Sanga of Mewar, Sultan Mahmud Khilji of Malwa and the founder of the Mughal empire in India, Babar — all walked its ramparts. The Moroccan traveller, Ibn Batutah, knew well the bazaars of Chanderi. History nestles quietly in the crumbling turrets, overpowered by the incense in the quaint shops at the base of the citadel. The lustre of the Chanderi sarees remains undiminished.

▲ *A view from the fort at sunset*

Narwar

arwar fort straddles the Vindhyan crests, a granite range overlooking a lazy bend in the Sindh river. Desolate and rugged, the monsoon-drenched ruins of crumbling palaces in the citadel look down on the cluttered town of Narwar, 400 feet below.

The classical name of Narwar is Nalapura, derived from Nala, the consort of the fabled beauty, Damayanti. It is said that Nala, descended from Kusha, son of Lord Rama, built the original fort. James Tod wrote (1978, p 280): 'Nurwar…We may…without hesitation, adopt…A.D. 295 for the period of Raja Nala, whose history is one of the grand sources of delight to the bards of Rajpootana…' Tod was drawn to *Dhola Maru re Duha*, the lyric and bardic tale of the chivalrous Dulha Rai, a twelfth century prince, who left his patrimony at Narwar and forged the way for the establishment of the house of Amber-Jaipur.

The twilight of legend and fact suggests that Narwar was a fortified settlement of the Nagas, their emergence in the third century coinciding with the Kushana decline. The Nagas were non-

Aryans; at their peak, they were dominant from Hastinapur to Vidisha. Narwar was part of the Gupta empire from the fourth to the sixth century. It became part of Harshvardhana's domains during the first half of the seventh century — the last of the Hindu kingdoms to qualify as pan-Indian. Kannauj was the capital, though Narwar's size and strength accorded it considerable autonomy.

Narwar was a cultural hub in the eighth century. The litterateur Bhavabhuti spent many years here. Narwar is believed by Alexander Cunningham to be Padmavati, the flourishing city of Bhavabhuti's ten-act romantic social play *Malati-Madhavam*, characters of which included Malati, daughter of Bhurivasu, a minister, and Madhavam, a young student and son of Devarata, a minister of

▼ *The Narwar hill fort on a Vindhyan crest overlooking the town of Narwar*

another state. Other characters in this drama portraying the day-to-day living of the times are Madayantika and Makaranda. Bhavabhuti's other works were *Mahavir Charitam* on Rama's early life and *Uttar Ramacharitam*, which portrayed Rama's return from exile and subsequent enthronement in Ayodhya.

Bhavabhuti's eminence in Sanskrit drama literature is second only to Kalidasa: he was often invited to the court of Yashovarman (720–750) in Kannauj. The king was an advocate of Vedic Hinduism, a patron of the arts, and progressive enough to depute emissaries to China, then under the T'ang dynasty (618–907) whose zenith coincided with Yashovarman's reign. The Varma dynasty of Yashovarman spanned the period from Harshvardhan's death (647) till the conquest of Kannauj (816) by the Pratihara Rajputs.

The Kachhwaha Rajput, Vajradaman, chief of Narwar, seized Gwalior from his Pratihara masters at the close of the tenth century. The Kachhwahas, with Narwar and Gwalior forts under their rule, became a separate entity; they withstood the Paramaras at Dhar and forestalled hostility from the Chandellas by recognising them as first-among-equals in the region. The Kachhwahas joined the Hindu confederacy under Jaipal I of Lahore against Mahmud of Ghazni (997–1030). The alliance was defeated. Later, the Kachhwahas acknowledged Mahmud's overlordship.

The Kachhwahas were chiefs of Narwar-Gwalior for about a century, when its lovelorn ruler, Dulha Rai, captive to his bride's beauty, left the domain in the care of a sister's son, a Pratihara,

who usurped the kingdom. Dulha Rai migrated from Narwar. Endowed with a generous dowry, a supportive father-in-law, some chicanery and much valour, he was able to establish a kingdom in Rajputana's Dhundhera region. Dulha Rai's son and successor, Kakil Dev, went on to draw the first contours of Amber.

◀ *Gwalior fort – its history was closely linked with Narwar's*

THE FORTS OF BUNDELKHAND

Inside Amber Fort, Rajasthan. Amber was the principal Kachhwaha Rajput kingdom from where branched Narwar's ruling dynasty in the sixteenth century. Both Akbar and Jehangir married princesses from Amber. Narwar's Kachhwahas helped the Mughals consolidate power in Bundelkhand

eanwhile, the Delhi Sultanate was consolidating. The Pratiharas of Narwar-Gwalior came under pressure when Iltumish (1211–36) besieged Gwalior in 1232, forcing its ruler Sarang Deo to take refuge in Narwar fort. In 1251, the Sultanate armies under Balban attacked Raja Chahada Deva who held Chanderi and Narwar. Enormous booty fell into Balban's hands. Chanderi and Narwar were annexed to the Sultanate's Malwa province. Timur's invasion in 1398 crippled the Sultanate, opportune for the Gwalior Tomars, who seized Narwar fort.

The Tomars reluctantly accepted Delhi's authority when the Sultanate steadied under the

Lodis, but gave offence by giving asylum (1502) to the Dholpur ruler, fleeing from the Sultan, Sikander Lodi (1489–1517). The Sultan launched an offensive on Narwar fort held by the Tomars. It was a protracted operation on the steep Vindhyan scarps. A Sultanate force was beaten back, as also reinforcements. The Sultan himself came, but had to retreat. The arduous siege ended only when the defenders were starved out. After the fort's capitulation in 1508, the Sultan ordered a general massacre.

The Sultan — though born of a Hindu mother, the daughter of a goldsmith — was given to bigoted frenzy. All the temples were destroyed. The Sultan stayed on to construct mosques and repair the city walls, and the Jhansi, Gwalior and Dabra gateways. The outer walls were extended to a circumference of ten miles commanded by a strengthened *bala hissar*, or inner citadel.

The Kachhwahas returned when Prince Askarn of Amber was installed at Narwar by the Sultan of Delhi, Islam Shah Sur (1545–55). This marked the coming alive of the Narwar–Amber trail, laid centuries earlier by Dulha Rai. Earlier, in 1547, Askarn had seized the Amber throne after slaying a brother. An elder brother, Bihari Mal, backed by Mewat's Afghan governor, Haji

▶ *Audience halls inside Narwar fort*

Khan, confronted Askarn, who stepped down. Amber was left to Bihari Mal. Haji Khan's interest was on account of his marriage to Bihari Mal's daughter. The Afghan, to prevent domestic discord, prevailed upon the Sultan to award Narwar to Askarn.

Narwar and Amber were now bonded in family. The two Kachhwaha brothers in Bundelkhand and Rajputana were together in making their submissions to Akbar. The Kachhwaha–Mughal proximity was further secured in wedlock when Bihari Mal sealed a relationship with Akbar through another daughter: this princess from Amber bore Salim, the next emperor. In Narwar, Askarn joined up with the Mughal operations to bridle Madhukar Shah of Orchha, and later accompanied Akbar's revenue minister Todar Mal to Bihar to quell a rebellion. Askarn was engaged in administrative reform parleys by the emperor, and Narwar fort emerged a beehive of activity.

Akbar visited the fort — headquarters of the Narwar *sarkar* of the Malwa province. The dense forests around Narwar provided the emperor opportunity to hunt elephant and tiger. The description in Alexander Dow's *The History of Hindostan* (1973, p 234) is vivid:

'...hunting one day on the way near Narwar, a great royal tygress with five young ones took the road before him. Akbar advanced to the animal, while his retinue stood trembling with fear and astonishment to behold the event. The king having meditated his blow, spurred on his horse towards the fierce tygress, whose eyes flamed with rage, and with one stroke of his sabre, cut her across the loins and stretched her dead upon the ground. The omrahs who were present, in excess of joy, ran to kiss his royal stirrup, and offer up their thanks to god for his preservation.'

During Akbar's reign, Narwar was visited by Father Monserrate, a Portuguese priest and

◀ *Carving of the Trinity at Hawa Paur on an ornate door-jamb*

▲ *The Alamgir Darwaza, named after Aurangzeb*

traveller, who was also tutor to the emperor's son Murad. The Jesuit was witness to the festivals of Holi and Moharram at Narwar; he commented on the surrounding areas being infested by robbers. (Ansari, 1975, p 3) Later, during Jehangir's time , an Englishman, William Finch, visited Narwar. He described the town to be one of considerable size, encircled by a wall. He also described the narrow pathway that led steeply to the fort, which according to him was well guarded by soldiers. (Ansari, 1975, p 34)

The Kachhwahas were vulnerable in Shahjehan's reign, having backed Prince Khusro's son Dawar Baksh against Prince Khurram in the Mughal struggle for succession after Jehangir's death. Khusro was the grandson of Amber's Raja Bhagwan Das through a daughter — the sister of Man Singh of Amber. Khurram, on becoming the Emperor Shahjehan, dispossessed Narwar's Kachhwaha chief of the fort. Aurangzeb restored the fort back to the Kachhwahas in consideration of their support and valour in Mughal military operations.

Narwar fort remained an important Mughal administrative centre, with the Kachhwahas as

▲ *The kutcherry and (left) baradari*

kiledars. Imperial troops were maintained and military hardware serviced. After the collapse of the Mughals, the Scindia became the overlord of Narwar. The Kachhwahas were resentful. Matters reached a head when Man Singh, a Kachhwaha — referred to as the 'Raja of Narwar' — was imprisoned in Gwalior fort. He escaped, fought the British in the 1857 uprising, but later fell into their hands. Man Singh ingratiated himself with his captors by betraying the revolutionary leader Tatya Tope and getting him trapped.

An imposing flight of steps leads into the fort. The Alamgiri Darwaza, named after Aurangzeb, is followed by an ascent to the Sayyidon ka Darwaza, so called because of repairs carried out by the Sayyid governor of the fort. And then, the Pir Darwaza. The climb becomes steeper till the Gaumukhi Darwaza is reached — the last gate on the ascent; it is also known as the Hawa Paur due to the invigorating gusts of wind at the fort entrance.

Vegetation peeps through the cracks. Where kings once ruled, cattle and the cowherds now reign. Vandalism is on display, with paving stones uprooted and stucco facings wrenched out. A two-acre square tank, thirty-feet deep and hewn out of a single rock, was the fort's main source of water, but it has been dry now for more than a century.

The buildings in the fort are a blend of Hindu and Muhammadan. The Mughals left their imprint in the fort through a simply-designed garden, which has four raised irrigation channels crossing at the centre. These channels divide the space into quarters. Geometric ordering of foliage, brimming waters and ablution tanks are in ample evidence at Narwar. The Mughals borrowed the idea of these 'paradise gardens' from Persia.

There is a Roman Catholic cemetery in the fort. The square-shaped walled-in cemetery encompasses some 10,000 square feet. From the eighteenth century, European artillerymen had come to be increasingly employed to train troops and cast guns. Crude iron was produced in the vicinity. The Portuguese as well as the Germans were given service in large number by the Mughals. The French were employed by the Scindia. The flaking walls of a small chapel are consumed by shrubbery. The remains of an altar can be identified, topped as it was by a cross. There are a number of tombs in the cemetery, including that of a German, Cornelius Oliver, who died in 1747. A Portuguese-inscribed stone can be seen. Another tombstone in Persian records the death of an eight-year-old European girl, Margharita — probably Portuguese — the daughter of a doctor.

A story is told about the Nats, a wandering tribe of rope performers, who avoid entering Narwar. Many hundreds of years ago, when the fort was beleaguered, the local chief needed to send a missive across. For the purpose, a rope was stretched out from the fort. But no one dared to walk on the rope, though the desperate chief promised half his kingdom. At last, a woman volunteered. She made the Raja repeat his promise in the presence of the courtiers. The Nat walked on the rope and delivered the letter. When she was returning, the Raja, to keep his possessions intact, cut the rope. The woman was killed in the fall. The Nats vowed never to enter the treacherous kingdom again.

▶ *The mint*

Kundar

The romance of Kundar fort is woven around the story of the Khangars — a community long scattered. It is a tale that has been pieced together through folk songs and archaeological remains on hillocks round-shouldered with age. This ninth-century fort is an invitation to muse on vanished dynasties and lost kingdoms.

The Khangar deity was Devi, the great goddess with a thousand faces and appellations; in Kundar, the embodiment was in Giddhvahini Devi, whose now quite elaborate shrine stands not far from the fort. The Khangars are still drawn to Kundar — the abandoned citadel's towers appear to exercise a strange psychic hold and its dungeons seem to conceal many mysteries.

Kundar looks radiant from afar. One moment its turrets are aglow in the sunlight, the next, hidden from view by the arc of a granite cliff or a bend in the path curving its way through chessboard fields. A rocky incline through the girdle of outer walls leads to a gateway paved with

◀ *A corner tower of the Kundar fort (above) central quadrangle*

uneven flagstones. A gallery of recessed arches leads into an open court. Octagonal corner towers are blended skilfully into the body of the fort, a three-tiered structure.

An assortment of geometrical forms and design permutations — quadrangles and corridors, pavilions, towers and ramparts — hold space in balance and harmony. The scalloped arches and carved angle brackets resolve themselves into endless embellishments, giving the austere masonry variety and depth.

The Khangars, among Bundelkhand's original inhabitants, were listed by James Tod (1978, p 99) as an 'aboriginal race', with any claims to Rajput lineage countered by their non-Aryan 'totemistic tribal structure' (Crooke, 1896, p 230). The Khangars, kindred to a wider world, subscribed to *gotras* or sects: the hathgotiyas (*hathi*: elephant), nahargotiyas (*nahar*: lion), naggotiyas (*naga*: serpent), bargotiyas (*bar*: banyan tree) and others. Despite the military achievements of the Khangars, their avowal to Rajput descent was tenuous.

Kundar fort was built by the Chandellas. It fell in the administrative province of Sirsagarh. In consideration of its strategic importance, Parmardidev, the Chandella chief, made Kundar the

headquarters of a separate province, while appointing Shiaju, a Paramara Rajput, as governor of the fort. His deputy was Khub Singh, a Khangar.

In 1182, Shiaju was killed in the battle of Sirsagarh, when Parmardidev was defeated by Prithviraj Chauhan. This was signal for Khub Singh to switch loyalty to the Chauhans and usurp the province from the Chandellas. Pressure on the Rajputs following Mohammad Ghori's invasion (1191-92), the emergence of the Delhi Sultanate (1206) and the Chandella decline, led to a period of power realignments enabling the Khangars to expand their territory.

◀ *Inner gate of the fort*

▲ *The main complex of the Kundar fort*

The Khangars were ferocious warriors. Merciless in their treatment of the vanquished, they accumulated cultivable lands and wealth. Khub Singh built a chain of small fortresses. His successor was Hurmat Singh, who furthered the dominance of the Khangars by playing off the Rajput *jagirdars* against each other.

It was a slight to the Bundela chief, Sohanpal, which caused Hurmat Singh's downfall. The Bundela governed his fief at Mahoni under the overlordship of the Khangars. Sohanpal sought help from Hurmat Singh against some kinsmen who had usurped Mahoni. The Khangar laughed off the Bundela's request. Sohanpal used all manner of entreaties, but to no avail.

Bundela servitude to the Khangars had always irked, but the final blow came when, having ignored his entreaties for assistance, Hurmat Singh sought the hand of Sohanpal's daughter for his son Nagadeva. Hurmat was keen to advance his standing in the social hierarchy by marrying

*◄ The Giddhavahini
Temple at Kundar*

into the Bundelas. The proposal enraged Sohanpal, but prudence prevailed. The Bundela accepted the proposal and agreed to the Khangar ceremonies, including the festivities at the groom's place.

The celebrations grew raucous with wine flowing freely in Kundar fort. The Khangars did not recognise Sohanpal's soldiers, disguised as retainers, creeping in from the shadows under the colourful festoons. What followed has been immortalised in Vrindavan Lal Verma's *Garh Kundar*. At night, as the revellers, inebriated with drugged wine, groped around in the fort, Sohanpal's men, sword in hand, struck. The Khangars and their chief fell where they stood.

Sohanpal took over Kundar, made it his capital, and abandoned the idea of repossessing Mahoni. A Paramara prince who had helped Sohanpal, was given the hand of the winsome Bundela princess. There were to be no Bundela marriage alliances with the Kachhwahas, Chauhans and Tomars, as they did not help against the Khangars. Sohanpal had probably promised his daughter to the other chieftains, too, who, when left unobliged, snapped their relationships with the Bundelas.

The legend goes that a Khangar princess who was pregnant, to escape the Bundelas, hid in a field of *kusum* — the thistle-like, dye-yielding flower — where she gave birth to a son. The woman, shielded initially by a fakir, was given refuge in a Dangi household, an off-the-mainstream community remotely related to the Rajputs. When the Bundela soldiers came looking, the Khangar's protectors denied her presence. The pursuers, to single out the Khangar, ferreted out all the women in the family, and asked them to eat *maheri* — rice in skimmed milk, sprinkled

with cumin, meant to be taken in family communion. To their credit, the Dangis did not flinch in having to eat *maheri* with a Khangar.

A bounty of tradition was generated. Dangi intrepidity to save a Khangar in distress led to a practice where the two communities together partake of *maheri* during celebrations. The Khangars, in remembrance, fashioned a deity in whose presence falsehood was abjured. Further, in deference to the cover provided by the kusum field during their ancestor's birth, the Khangars forswore apparel dyed with this crop. Fakirs, normally receivers of alms,

▶ *A pujari preparing for the day at the Giddhavahini Temple*

◄ The outer entrance to the Kundar fort

act as providers in a Khangar wedding and bring presents.

There is another version: according to the Khangars, the feud was not between the Khangar ruler and his Bundela tributary; rather, the adversaries were two *jagirdars* — the Khangar's son sought the hand of the Bundela's daughter. The resultant bloodletting led to the liquidation of the Khangar *jagirdar* and the usurpation of his lands by the Bundelas, but without impacting on the ruling Khangar dynasty. The Khangars remained masters of Kundar till they were dethroned by the Sultan of Delhi, Muhammad Tughlak.

The Sultan sought the hand of the princess Kesar Devi, sister of the Khangar ruler, Bardai Singh. The Sultan was cold-shouldered, and responded by besieging the fort. According to the Khangars, the other clans, including the Bundelas, did not help. When the situation became hopeless, the Khangars prepared for *jauhar*. The event is cited to buttress the affinity Khangars claim to have with Rajput rituals. For the beleaguered, self-destruction was preferred to surrender and dishonour. Women in their finery jumped into a pyre. Children, too, were consigned to the flames. The men died in battle harness. After the battle, the Sultan handed Kundar over to the Bundelas to administer.

◄ A well preserved pavilion with arches and brackets

Even centuries after the Khangars fell, during the investiture ceremonies of Datia's Bundela kings, a model of Kundar fort used to be broken. This was to demonstrate Bundela hostility against the Khangars. Bundela expansion and consolidation from Mahoba to Seondha was sporadic, factored into the fluctuating strength of the Delhi Sultanate and the anarchy inflicted by Timur's invasion. In 1482, the Bundela chief Malkhan Singh (1468–1501) came into direct conflict with Sultan Bahlol Lodi (1451–89) over Kalpi. The Mughals arrived in 1526. The new chief Rudra Pratap (1501–31) decided to move the Bundela capital from Kundar to a safer location.

The Bundelas shifted to Orchha. The *baolies* at Kundar became the haunt of bats, and weeds and creepers overtook the pavilions. The underground chambers, once lit by torches, lie still and sombre. The silence and the isolation magnifies each sound, even the wind blowing through the grass which covers the wounds of centuries.

▼ *A maze of underground dungeons*

THE FORTS OF BUNDELKHAND

Mahoba

The *Mahoba Khand* of Chand Bardai's *Prithviraj Raso* portrays the pulsating tempo of the epic conflict between the Chauhans of Delhi and the Chandellas. It was Prithviraj Chauhan's triumph over Parmardideva of Mahoba in 1182 that triggered the Chandella decline. The clash of the titans fractured the Rajput polity irrevocably. This was a watershed in the history of India: the weakening of the indigenous military capacity led to the victory of Mohammad Ghori over Prithviraj in 1192 and the foundation of the Delhi Sultanate in 1206.

From smouldering Mahoba arose the saga of Alha and Udal. These Banaphar Rajput youths fought, alongside the Chandellas, the losing battle against the Chauhans. The two brothers came from Chilla, a landing *ghat* on the Yamuna, still in use on the northern edge of Bundelkhand. It was Mahoba's court bard Jagnik Rao, whose *Alha Khand* ensured immortality for the two chivalrous warriors.

The bards, whether Chand Bardai or Jagnik Rao, were flashy chroniclers. They wove the tales of their royal patrons into colourful renditions. In Bundelkhand, song and verse extolling heroic deeds came to be known as *alhas*, and were rendered in a distinctive style. *Alhas*, accompanied by the dholak and the refrain of an *alaap*, still resound from the hillocks on commemorative occasions.

The Chandellas, it is believed, were descended from Hemavati, the beautiful daughter of Hemraj, priest of the Raja of Kashi. Legend has it that the moon-god Chandrama could not resist her as she bathed in the shimmering waters of a lotus-filled pond. A distraught Hemavati cursed Chandrama, who consoled his consort that the son of their union would be the lord of the earth from whom would sprout a thousand branches.

Chandrama disclosed that their son would be born on the banks of the Karnavati river and reign in Mahoba. He would possess the *parasmani* or philosopher's stone and build a fort on the hill of Kalinjar. At the child's birth, Chandrama performed a great festival, the *mahotsava*, from which Mahoba derived its name. The festival was attended by all the gods. This was the eleventh day of the waxing moon of Vaisakhi. The festival and its traditions still continue.

The horoscope of the newborn Chandravarman was written by Vrihaspati. When sixteen, the prince killed a tiger. He became a powerful monarch and designated Mahoba as his chief city.

Closer to reality, it has been surmised that Chandravarman was a Gond chief — the Chandellas were an indigenous people who rose towards ennoblement. Durgavati of Gondwana, the valiant sixteenth-century queen, was a Chandella married to a Gond.

▶ *Mahoba town as seen from the fort*

THE FORTS OF BUNDELKHAND

The Chandellas were tributaries of the Kannauj Pratiharas in the eighth century. This power equation was disturbed when the Deccan Rashtrakutas invaded Bundelkhand early in the ninth century, an opportunity used by the Chandella chief Nannuka to drive out the Pratiharas and set up capital in the walled city of Khajuraho, thirty-four miles south of Mahoba. Nannuka became the first Chandella king, ruling from 831 to 845. The wresting of Chanderi from Bhojdeva of Kannauj (836–885) by the Chandellas, boosted the standing of this fledgling dynasty.

Mahoba developed in Rahilya's time (900–915), though Khajuraho remained the epicentre. Alberuni, who accompanied Mahmud of Ghazni on his expeditions, writes about Khajuraho, as does Ibn Batutah, who came in 1335. An early Chandella landmark in Mahoba is the granite temple of Rahilya — the sun god. The original sculpture, which was in the *aradhana mudra*, overlooked the Rahilya Sagar, an irrigation lake built as a welfare measure.

Chandella influence extended when Rahilya's daughter married into the neighbouring Chedis and his son and successor Harsha (915–930) took a bride from Sambhar's Chauhans. It was further strengthened when Yashovarman (930–950) took Kalinjar. This celebrated fort had recently been taken by the Rashtrakutas from the Kannauj Pratiharas. Yashovarman provided critical help to the Pratiharas against the Rashtrakutas, from whom Kalinjar was recovered. The Chandellas kept the fort; they also acquired, from the Pratiharas, an idol of Vishnu, originally with the King of Bhot or Tibet, for which a temple was constructed at Khajuraho.

Dhangadev (950–1008) — one of the greatest Chandellas — was part of a confederation led

by Jaipal of Lahore, against Ghazni. He kept in check the Palas and the Rashtrakutas. Victories were glorified and villages donated to maintain the families of those who died in battle. Dhangadev's passion and intensity can be perceived from

◀ *Temple of Rahilya – the sun god*

▲ *Khajuraho, the cultural standard bearer. Mahoba, the administrative capital, and Khajuraho were the two principal Chandella cities*

the unrivalled profusion of carvings and richness of sculptures in the Kandariya Mahadeo and Vishwanath temples he built at Khajuraho. On reaching 100 years of age, Dhangadev immolated himself on burning cow dung cakes at the Prayag *sangam*.

Vidyadhara (1017–30) attempted to forge an understanding with Kannauj to meet the threat of Mahmud of Ghazni. The initiative failed. Piqued and apprehensive, Vidyadhara sent a son to confront the Kannauj ruler, Rajpal. Tempers flared, swords flashed, and Rajpal was killed. Vidyadhara shifted base from Khajuraho to Mahoba as Mahmud drew closer. The invader's objective was Kalinjar, but the stronghold stood up to him on two occasions. When the threat of Mahmud receded, Vidyadhara seized large chunks of the *doab* from Kannauj.

Kirtivarman gained both from the Kalachuris and the Chedis. The Chandella star continued to shine with Madanvarman (1125-65). He subdued Malwa's Paramaras and held off the Chalukyans in the Deccan. Jainism was patronised, pilgrim resthouses built and hectic work

▲ *Dargah of Pir Mubarak Shah from Herat – the present keeper or sajjad-e-nasheen is a direct descendant of the Pir*

meet with a violent death. I was…witness to… this old belief. In February 1843… the brother of the Chhatrpur Raja, was obliged to go to Naugaon to celebrate his daughter's marriage, as he did not dare to have a wedding procession with music through the city which the ghosts of the old Chandel Rajas were believed to haunt.' Muhammad Ghori's invasions came soon,

▶ *Mosque at the site of Parmardideo's palace – an inscription in Persian dated 1322 praises the Delhi Sultan, Ghiyas-ud-din Tughlak*

sweeping away the Delhi Chauhans. This allowed Parmardideva to retrieve Mahoba, but it could only be a weak control, as the Turko-Afghans were well on course to establishing the Sultanate under Qutub-ud-din Aibak, Muhammad Ghori's general. The Chandellas reconciled themselves to being tributaries. But, after Parmardideva's death in 1202, his minister Aja Deo refused to pay tribute. The following year the Turko-Afghans ransacked Mahoba.

A *subehdar* was appointed at Mahoba, accountable to the Sultanate. Over the years, the Mewatis, Gonds, Khangars and the Bundelas occupied Mahoba. Timur's invasion in 1398 loosened Delhi's hold over Mahoba till the revival of the Sultanate's central authority by the Lodis. Under

Mughal administration, Mahoba became an administrative unit controlled from Kalinjar, part of the province of Allahabad. Mahoba, comprising 82,000 *bighas*, was among the more prosperous Mughal possessions in Bundelkhand.

The Mughals were fascinated by Mahoba's *paan*, or betel leaf, from the fragile creeper nurtured by the earliest Chandellas. Its leaf, taken with the right ingredients, was also known for its aphrodisiac qualities. Mahoba's folded *paan* leaf, or *beda* — seductively fastened with a clove — got its sharp, juicy characteristics and

▶ *Chandika Devi Temple – among the earliest (ninth century) Chandella temples. It is the site of the mahotsava from which Mahoba took its name*

aroma from a special manure prepared with *jowar* flour, mustard oil cakes, curd and cow dung. The choicest of *paan* selections were included in the tribute paid to the Mughal emperor.

Of the Chandella fortifications in Mahoba, only some impressions remain, which overlook the town. The old fort area is identified by the remnants of the Bhainsasur and Bheetarkot *darwazas*. The cultural crosscurrents are evident: the thirteenth-century *dargah* of a saint from Herat, Pir Mubarak Shah, lies some distance from a rock-cut tenth-century Shiva in *tandava*; the Kaal Bhairava, a Maniya Devi temple, a shrine of Hanuman; and *havan kunds* for *yajnas*.

The Madan Sagar is on the southern side, its scenic splendour heightened by two temples built on islets in the lake — the granite Kakra Math devoted to Shiva, and a Vishnu temple, now in ruin. Dipping into the Madan Sagar is the grey granite of a fortified hill, the silence broken only by the twitter of water birds gliding past a mélange of *ghats* and temples. In the east of the town

◀ *Temple of Maniya Devi in Mahoba (ninth century). The goddess is also recognised by the Gonds as their deity*

▲ *Baithak of Indal (Alha's son) on the Madan Sagar*

is the Vijay Sagar built by Vijay Pala (1030–1040), taking advantage of a shallow valley.

The Kirti Sagar embankment is the site of the Kajli fair in August, a celebration of the monsoons, wellbeing and fidelity. Centuries ago, Prithviraj Chauhan's men had attacked the royal Kajli procession, elaborate with decorated palanquins, elephants and artists. The intruders were repulsed, but the celebrations traditionally earmarked to coincide with Raksha Bandhan, had to be postponed. Accordingly, Kajli came to be celebrated on the day after Raksha Bandhan.

A *baithak* survives on the Kirat Sagar. This is where the Chandella kings relaxed with their consorts, critiqued the arts and appraised performances. A favourite was the *Prabodha-chandrodaya* encapsulating Vedanta philosophy in drama form. The celestial Chandella setting — with images of Khajuraho — was embellished by offerings from Mahoba's betel creeper encircling the areca palm, complete with the ambrosial waft of a *supari* nut in a *paan* leaf.

▶ *Baithak on the Kirat Sagar*

Ajaigarh

The mighty fort of Ajaigarh crowns a flat spur of the Vindhyan range. The ninth-century fort derived its name from Ajaipala, a sage who lived on the hill Kedar Parvat. Ajaigarh provided a safe haven for the Chandellas after their capital Mahoba was taken by Prithviraj Chauhan of Delhi in 1182. Internecine Rajput warring catalysed Muslim invasions and conquests in India. The Chauhan dynasty was extinguished in 1192 by Muhammad Ghori. His general, Qutub-ud-din Aibak, founder of the Delhi Sultanate, conquered Mahoba in 1203, which led to Ajaigarh emerging as an administrative centre. The fort pulsated for a century-and-a-half, with whatever remained of Chandella splendour.

The hill, of granite and sandstone, is steep. Rock inscriptions abound, relating mainly to the later Chandella period: from Madanvarman in the mid-twelfth century till the reign of Parmardideva's great grandson Viravarman in the late thirteenth century. Chandella territory was confined now to the tract near Kalinjar, Panna and Ajaigarh.

Ajaigarh fort, at an elevation of 800 feet from the plains, allowed the Chandellas to recoup following their debilitating battles. The formidable bastions and stout corner towers indicate that the fort was built to withstand prolonged sieges. The stronghold was self-contained, with a good water supply. It could shelter large populations. The hills — dense with sal and tendu — further strengthened the defences of the fort.

A sheer climb leads to the north entrance, the Kalinjar Darwaza, which faces in the direction of Kalinjar fort twenty miles away. Another gateway, on the southeast, is the Tarhaoni Darwaza, which overlooks a village of the same name. The other three gateways are blocked. The Ken river can be seen in the distance, silvery and sinuous.

The thick battlemented outer wall of the fort, three miles in circumference, girdles a triangular tract. The uneven rampart, composed of huge blocks of stones, never has the same breadth or depth for more than a few yards running. In the parapets, beautifully carved pillars and doorjambs torn from Hindu and Jain temples were set haphazardly by the Muhammadan *kiledars.*

At the Kalinjar Darwaza is a dancing Ganesha with lines so lyrical that one can almost hear the ankle bells. Close by, two huge caverns, the Ganga and Yamuna, hewn in rock and replenished from an underground stream, comprise an important water source. Varaha, an incarnation of Vishnu, recreates Earth's salvation. A colossal Shantinath signals the pervasive Jain presence in Bundelkhand.

Among the rock-cut images near the Tarhaoni Darwaza is a panel of *sapta-matrikas* or seven

▶ *The dancing Ganesha at the Kalinjar Darwaza*

◀ *Rock carvings depicting obeisance to Shiva linga*

mother-goddesses, accompanied by Veer-bhadra, a form of Shiva. This is a reminder of the Shakti cult which flourished in the fort. Other inscriptions in rock include a cow and calf, a human palm and a child in the lap of a goddess — all symbols of fecundity. Nearby, there is a sombre setting of sati pillars. The memorials bear the symbols of the crescent moon and the sun. The female hand denotes a blessing upon the sati.

A cluster of temples overlooks the languid waters of a *talao* named after Parmardideva and

▼ *A cove with secular and religious carvings*

▶ *Parmardideva Talao – where women from the royal family bathed*

used by women of the royal household. This pristine setting in the southern area of the fort is interspersed by an illusory, fleeting vision of Parmardideva's wife, a fabled beauty.

Tier upon tier of elaborately carved stones rise in a gentle taper in Ajaigarh's temples. Craftsmen — who worshipped the rising sun as the mystic world lotus — have carved its petals on the pillars, arches and the soaring *shikharas* of these temples. Panels and friezes are decorated with the figures of voluptuous nymphs and celestial *apsaras*.

Congregations in the fort's centre, on the edge of the Ajaipal Talao, break into folk songs from the *Alha Khand*. The warriors Alha and Udal were an exceptional theme, considering that the usual bardic effort centred around kings who were regarded as akin to gods and descendants of celestial beings. Chand Bardai, in *Prithviraj Raso*, composed eulogies about the Chauhan king of Delhi; he also wrote about the impious transgressions of his master's foe, Parmardideva, leading to Mahoba's grim fate and the fall of the Chandellas.

Nothing has changed at the Parmardideva Talao since the Bengal Army's Captain W.R. Pogson's visit to Ajaigarh. He described the fort as 'stupendous' in his *History of the Boondelas* published in 1828. Earlier, the 1809 edition of the Asiatic Annual Register, quoted by Pogson had recorded:

'...the ruins of three magnificent Hindoo temples, built of stones, laid without cement, but most nicely fitted to each other, and adorned within and without, with sculpture, of chaste design, and the most exquisite workmanship. The era of the erection of these venerable buildings is lost in antiquity; but they are evidently much older than the fortress...' (1974, p135)

Adjacent to the Ajaipala Talao, now under water hyacinths, is an ancient statue of black stone worshipped as Ajaipala. The story is told of a British commandant who threw the idol into the water. The commandant became violently ill and the image had to be restored with honour to its shrine. It was also believed that a stone from the sacred compound of this temple, if placed in a home, would ward off the evil eye.

Vestiges of the Chandella dynasty continued at Ajaigarh till Akbar took the fort, then under a Gond *kiledar*. At about the same time, the Mughals also wiped out the Gondwana kingdom governed by Rani Durgavati. Of Chandella lineage, she opted to resist the emperor and stabbed herself to death after getting wounded in battle. This spirit of defiance remained alive: some three centuries later, Durgavati's descendant, Raja Shankar Shah of the Gond royal family of Garhmandla and his son, revolutionaries of 1857, were tied to cannons and blown up by the British.

Abul Fazl's records refer to Ajaigarh as the headquarters of a *mahal* in the Kalinjar *sarkar*. The Mughal writ ran here till the entry of Champat Rai and his son Chhatrasal, whose Panna became the dominant principality in Bundelkhand towards the end of Aurangzeb's reign. Champat Rai had fought on Aurangzeb's side against Dara Shikoh in the decisive battle of Samugarh during the Mughal civil war of succession. He had also deftly piloted the combined armies of Aurangzeb and Murad Baksh in difficult terrain and across dangerous fords in the Chambal area.

Champat Rai fell out with Aurangzeb after the latter's ascent to the Mughal throne. The Bundela was upset by the emperor's bigotry and needless threats. Champat Rai blocked Mughal access to Malwa, his guerrilla tactics well complemented by the thickly wooded region. But the insurgency could not be sustained. Chased by the Orchha troops, and hemmed in by a group of hostile Dhandera Rajputs, Champat Rai stabbed himself to death along with his wife. His son Chhatrasal (b.1649, d.1731) entered Mughal military service.

Chhatrasal was offered the *kiledari* of Satara. But his ambitions prevailed. The Bundela chief left the

◀ *Ajaigarh fort – Chandella legacy*

▲ *Ajaipala's Talao*

Mughals and linked up with the Marathas. He met Chhatrapati Shivaji and stayed with him at Pune for a few days. An over-cautious Shivaji could not bring himself to fully trust Chhatrasal. Rather than enter into an alliance, he counselled that Chhatrasal step up his independent activity in Bundelkhand. Chhatrasal assaulted Ajaigarh fort in 1674. He was successful and confirmed in his possessions by the emperor.

Ajaigarh was inherited (1732) as part of Jaitpur state by Chhatrasal's son, Jagat Raj. After him, a family settlement saw Ajaigarh, along with Banda, bestowed to a nephew Guman Singh (1765-81), who died leaving a minor son in the charge of his army commander Arjun Singh. An alliance of 'king-maker' Himmat Bahadur's mercenary army and the Peshwa's protégé Ali Bahadur attacked and killed Arjun Singh. Ali Bahadur became the Nawab of Banda in 1791 and, following a siege of six weeks, took Ajaigarh fort in 1800. Ajaigarh's protection allowed Ali Bahadur's cavalry to run loose, raising taxes effectively from Panna, Bijawar, Charkhari and Jaitpur for the Peshwa.

The Ajaigarh–Pune political bridge could be traced back to Mastani. She was Chhatrasal's gift to Peshwa Baji Rao I (1720–41). Their relationship resulted in a love child, Shamsher Bahadur, the father of Ali Bahadur. Shamsher Bahadur succumbed to wounds received in the third battle of Panipat (1761). Ali Bahadur died (1802) besieging Kalinjar; his son, also named Shamsher Bahadur, was in Pune, at the side of Peshwa Baji Rao II, at the time. He rushed back to Bundelkhand, imprisoned a usurping relative in Ajaigarh fort and poisoned him.

However, the balance of power was shifting with the mercenary, Himmat Bahadur, switching over to the side of the British, and Lakshman Daoowa — a notorious freebooter, and no friend of the Marathas — with British connivance, bribing the Ajaigarh *kiledar* into surrendering the fort to him. Daoowa terrorised the surroundings from the heights of Ajaigarh. This brought him into

conflict with the British, who were seeking an understanding with the Bundelas to isolate and further weaken the Peshwa. The Maratha's power was already declining, reflected also in the Treaty of Bassein, 1802.

In 1809, the British decided to take Ajaigarh. The campaign, under Colonel Martindale, lasted a month. The encounters were fierce. The British carried artillery to an adjacent hilltop commanding the gates of Ajaigarh. Ambushes in the precipitous hills resulted in heavy casualties before Daoowa capitulated. According to the Asiatic Annual Register of 1809 (in Pogson, 1974, p 136):

'The batteries opened at day break on the 12th of February 1809 and so heavy and destructive was the fire, that the enemy could not shew a man, and fired in the intervals while our guns were cooling. By sunset two of their guns were dismounted and three of the gates, with their defences, laid in ruins. Immense masses of stone and masonry were brought down. Next morning, the batteries played on the upper gate and defences with powerful effect, and at noon the enemy displayed a white flag. At four they evacuated the fort; and at five we occupied it.'

Lakshman Daoowa fled to Calcutta leaving his family, eight in all, in the charge of his father-

Chandella temple at Ajaigarh – with ornate mandappa pillars and a sumptuously carved entrance to the sanctum

▲ *Chandella temples now in ruins*

in-law who lived in a village at the base of the fort. The old man slit the throats of the entire family, as well as his own.

Ajaigarh's political and military developments at the turn of the eighteenth century illustrated well the raison d'etre for entrepreneurial soldiering in Bundelkhand, represented by Himmat Bahadur, well stocked with cannon, armed men and a Danish commander: Colonel Meiselback. A brahmin gosain, Himmat Bahadur's real name was Anupgiri. He was brought up in the foster care of the Jhansi *kiledar*. These were disturbed times, when religion-oriented groups — bairagis, gosains, nagas, sanyasis — banded together in order to influence events, the prime interest being self-preservation.

Himmat Bahadur was ready to be hired, whether by Oudh, the Marathas or the British. This mercenary had managed the *doab* revenues on behalf of Nawab Shuja-ud-daula of Oudh, whose life he reputedly saved in the Battle of Buxar against the British. He served Mahadji Scindia, before aligning with the Peshwa for securing Bundelkhand through Ali Bahadur. Himmat Bahadur transferred his allegiance again to consolidate the British in Bundelkhand. A grateful Governor-General, Lord Wellesley (1798–1805) rewarded Himmat Bahadur with a generous *jagir*. The East India Company took Meiselback into service and made him a brigade-commander.

The British handed over Ajaigarh fort to Raja Bakth Singh, a nephew of the erstwhile ruler Guman Singh. Ajaigarh was recognised as a princely state in return for allegiance through a *sanad* agreement. Banda became a district in British India.

Today Ajaigarh fort lies lonely, crumbling and covered with creepers. Forlorn peacocks find refuge in the abandoned ruins of what was once a mighty Chandella stronghold.

Of the known and countless unknown who made Bundelkhand's history, one was Lieutenant W. Jamieson, shot through both his thighs during the last battle of Ajaigarh. He is remembered by a reflective Captain Pogson recalling the farewell of Oliver Goldsmith's Vicar of Wakefield to his son:

'Go, and if you fall, though distant, exposed, and unwept by those that love you — the most precious tears are those with which heaven bedews the tomb of a soldier.'

– (as quoted by W.R. Pogson in *History of the Boondelas*, 1828)

▲ *Ajaigarh fort faces Kalinjar fort, on a spur twenty miles away*

Kalinjar

A solemnity shrouds Kalinjar. Ruined temples, palace remains and sculptures lie scattered in what was once the mightiest fort in mediaeval India. The hill on which the fort stands has been a *mahatirth* since ancient times. Hermits and ascetics, seers and sages still live and meditate here. The Vedas describe Kalinjar as a *tapasyasthana* for austere devotion. The Mahabharata proclaims that whosoever takes a dip in the lake of the gods at Kalinjar, achieves goodness equal to the gift of a thousand cows.

Kalinjar was a Chandella stronghold, described by Ferishta, the Bijapur historiographer, as unparalleled in strength. The citadel successfully withstood Mahmud of Ghazni. The Sultan, during one of his seventeen expeditions to India, marched menacingly towards Kalinjar (1019) when he was met by a Chandella army comprising 36,000 horses,

◀ *Principal entrance to the Kalinjar fort*
▶ *Approach to the Neelkantha Temple*

THE FORTS OF BUNDELKHAND

153

45,000 footmen and 640 elephants. Mahmud pillaged the countryside, but saw the fruitlessness of making a serious attempt on the citadel itself. The invader felt compelled to withdraw.

The windswept Kalinjar haunted the Sultan. He returned, unable to resist the challenge of the fort's rock face and the ramparts hanging on the edge of the scarps. An offensive was mounted in 1022. Again, Mahmud failed. The Sultan allowed himself to be appeased with the elephants, gold and jewels gifted by the Chandella king, Vidyadhara, along with some verses in praise. The Sultan's obsession with Kalinjar saved Khajuraho, exposed in open territory, not much distant from the path taken by Ghazni's ravaging cavalry.

Situated on Kalinjar hill, 900 feet high, the grim fort appears to have grown organically out of harsh rock. Anchored to the precipitous slopes are crenellated, grey, serpentine walls, the parapets relentlessly pursuing the hill's contours over a four-mile periphery. Parallel to its significance as a fort, the legend of Kalinjar's divinity has perpetuated. Kalinjar (*kal*: time; *jar*: destroy) is exalted as the abode of Shiva in the Koorma Purana, and is mentioned in the Padma Purana as among the nine holy spots in northern India. The Puranas, eighteen in total, supplement the Vedas as a corpus of Hindu beliefs, moral-philosophy and religion.

The hill was first fortified around 2000 years ago, though there had been earlier settlements in the area. The second century Roman scholar, Ptolemy, refers to Kalinjar as 'Kanagora', when it was under the Kushanas (in *Uttar Pradesh District Gazetteer of Banda*, 1988, p 34). The killing of the ruler of the kingdom, Kalinjarapura, in battle, and the conquest of Kalinjar fort in the third century (248–249) marked a milestone event — it flagged off the Kalachuri era. The victors, perhaps, were the forbearers of the Chedi Kalachuris. The conqueror came to be known as 'Kalinjaradhipati', or 'Lord of Kalinjar', a title of the early Kalachuri rulers.

Kalinjar fort changed hands from the Kalachuris to the Rashtrakutas in the eighth century,

▶ *Mahasadashiva, a form of Shiva, hewn out of rock*

followed by the Pratiharas in the ninth, and later, the Chandellas. There is evidence of the Rashtrakuta, Dantidurga (733–738), holding Kalinjar, and the Pratiharas, Nagabhata II (800–825) and Bhojdeva (836–885). The Rashtrakutas, aided by the Kalachuris, retook the fort from the Pratiharas, though only for a short period. The Chandellas came to the aid of their former masters, the Pratiharas, against the Rashtrakutas. They captured Kalinjar, pushed back the Rashtrakutas and helped the Pratiharas to recoup. The Chandella king, Yashovarman, kept Kalinjar for himself. This placed his dynasty in a strong enough position to deal with Mahmud of Ghazni.

Chandella power suffered a blow in the exhausting struggle against the Delhi Chauhans towards the close of the twelfth century. This paved the way for Qutub-ud-din Aibak's seizure of Kalinjar from the greatly weakened Chandellas in 1203. The old walls saw much blood and fire, and the garrison was forced to surrender as the fort's water supply ran dry. A contemporary chronicler Hasan Nizami recorded in the *Taj-ul- Ma'sir*:

'The garrison, in an extreme state of weakness and distraction, came out of the fort, and by compulsion left their native place empty, and the fort of Kalanjar, which was celebrated throughout the world for being as strong as the wall of Alexander, was taken. The temples were converted into mosques and abodes of goodness, and the ejaculations of the bead counters and the voices of the summoners to prayer ascended to the highest heaven, and the very name of idolatry was annihilated. Fifty thousand men came under the collar of slavery, and the plain became black as pitch with Hindus. Elephants and cattle, and countless arms, also became the spoil of the victors.' (Cunningham, 1969, p 25)

Hasan Nizami's account, in Persian, was an official history of the Delhi Sultanate, written on orders of Qutub-ud-din Aibak (1206-11). Such scribes employed by the Sultans were fervent in *Darul Islam*; their sole aim being to glorify the faith. They referred to the destruction of temples and killings of 'infidels' without intellectual or moral compunction. Often, there was exultant description of the tyrannies perpetrated in the name of religion. The Chandellas and other Hindu kingdoms of the era were unable to comprehend the intensity of the *mujahids* and the *ghazis*, which led to the Muslim conquests in India, described by Will Durant in his *The Story of Civilization* as 'probably the bloodiest story in history.' (1935, p 459)

Eka Mukhi Shivalinga carving at the Neel Kantha Temple

▲ *Gajataka Shiva destroying Gajasura*

The occupation of Kalinjar by the Turko-Afghans did not last long. The Chandellas re-established their authority over the stronghold to resume their hostile independence. But the dynasty's days of glory were over, left as they were with only Kalinjar and Ajaigarh. Kalinjar provided the Chandellas cover enough to exert their presence towards the east, in Baghelkhand.

After Aibak, Sultan Iltumish's commandant of Bayana and Gwalior, Malik Tayasai, made a futile attempt on Kalinjar. He retreated booty-laden after devastating the countryside, but without the fort. Sultan Nasir-ud-din's father-in-law and chief minister, Balban, plundered the territory around Kalinjar. Balban, later to succeed as Sultan (1266-87), was harsh, and the Chandellas acceded to a tributary status while remaining *kiledars* of the fort.

Early in the sixteenth century, the Lodis occupied Kalinjar. The Chandellas regained possession when the Lodis were crushed by the Mughals at Panipat (1526). After Babar ascended, his son Humayun attacked the fort. The siege was abandoned when Babar died. Humayun resumed the offensive after a few months, but gave up in the face of the spirited defence put up by the Chandella keepers of the fort.

Sher Shah, the Afghan king of the Sur dynasty in Delhi, who had driven Humayun from India to Persia, was successful at Kalinjar, but only after a siege lasting a year. On his way to the fort, Sher Shah was engaged in battle by Bharati Chand of Orchha — a fruitless intervention. Kirat Singh, the last of the Chandella rulers, was in possession of Kalinjar. Sher Shah's resolve and the severity of his offensive was triggered by Kirat's refusal to surrender a local chieftain who had ignored a summons to attend court in Delhi. The two adversaries, Afghans and Chandellas, both took a savage battering.

The Sultan was mortally wounded — hideously burnt by a fire-arrow rocket shell, which ricocheted after igniting an ammunition dump. According to Sir Wolseley Haig's account :

'…when the parallels had approached the walls, Sher Shah ascended a high tower in the line of circumvallation, ordered one of his officers to bring a supply of loaded shells, or…rockets, and amused himself in the meantime by shooting arrows into the town.. one of them was fired against the gate of the town, but rebounded and fell into and ignited a heap of ammunition by which the king was standing. Sher Shah was most severely burned…he summoned his nobles and commanded them to capture the fortress…' (1971, p 55)

The commanders were shaken by the Sultan's condition, but recovered soon enough to put in everything they could. The closing moments, described in the *Tarikh-i-Sher Shahi* by Abbas Khan Sarwani, an Afghan historian in Akbar's court (in Cunningham, 1969, p 26):

'…Men came and swarmed out instantly on every side like ants and locusts, and by the time of afternoon prayers captured the fort, putting everyone to the sword and sending all the infidels to hell. About the hour of evening prayers the intelligence of the victory reached Sher Shah, who lay on his countenance. Raja Kirat Singh, with seventy men remained in a house.

Kutub Khan the whole night long watched the house in person lest the Raja should escape. Sher Shah said to his sons that none of his nobles need watch the house, so that the Raja escaped out of the house, and the labour of this long watching was lost. The next day at sunrise, however, they took the Raja alive...'

Kirat Singh was executed and the Chandella dynasty in Bundelkhand came to an end. Sher Shah's son Islam Shah was crowned at Kalinjar. Some twenty years later, Kirat Singh's widowed daughter Durgavati gave her life in Gondwana defending her late husband's kingdom against Akbar's forces. She is remembered as Durgavati of Gondwana.

The Sur dynasty (1540–55) in Delhi was short-lived, and Kalinjar came under the rule of the Baghel Rajputs of Rewa — but not for long. After the reinstatement of Mughal rule in Delhi, Akbar's armies, under Majnun Khan Qaqushal, surrounded the fort. The defendants preferred to surrender (1569), aware of the fate of the other strongholds taken by assault. Kalinjar became the headquarters of a Mughal *sarkar* and part of the *jagir* of Birbal, a favourite of the emperor.

Chhatrasal of Panna captured Kalinjar (1688) from the Mughal *kiledar* Karam Ilahi. The Bundela chief appointed a Brahmin, Mandhata Chaube, as

◀ *Ganesha, in a standing pose – facing the Neel Kantha temple*

the fort's keeper. His descendants continued to administer the fort till it remained with Chhatrasal. Ali Bahadur, Maratha warlord of Banda, attacked Kalinjar with a siege that lasted two years. Ali Bahadur died at Kalinjar after a fall (1802) and the Marathas were warded off.

Kalinjar emboldened its occupants to plunder the surrounding British territory. In retaliation, the British attacked (1812) Kalinjar with two cavalry regiments and seven infantry battalions under Colonel Martindale who occupied a hill to the north of the fort. With considerable effort, four eighteen-pounders and two mortars were carried to the top. The surface was bare and earth had to be carried in canvas bags to mount the guns. The firing deflected off the walls. After a thorough survey of the defences, the British detected a vulnerable spot and directed concentrated fire for three weeks, causing a breach.

The British noted :

'We continued for several days to batter at the wall; mean time, the people in the fort gave us

▲ *Temple of Venkata Behari – among the Bundela remnants after Chhatrasal's takeover*

little interruption. Until we began to fire from our batteries, they had not fired a shot; this was from an old Indian point of honour, that it did not become a fort to fire until it was fired upon. After they did begin, they did no harm; they had only some old cannon, that were more dangerous to those that worked them, than to us...'
(Pogson, 1974, p 141)

Although their firearms were evidently of not much use, the defenders found another way to strike back. They wreaked havoc on the British by rolling boulders down the chasms. Every stone that was thrown or displaced brought down a heap of rubble, which sent the troops reeling back, blinded and suffocated by dust and smoke. Ultimately, in a compromise, the *kiledar* transferred the fort to the British for land in three villages in the plains. Remains of Chaube's residence and sundry *dharmashalas* can be seen in the fort.

The hill on which the fort stands is visible from afar. The rugged battlements are pockmarked with old wounds, from where the artillery has torn away the masonry.

▲ *Neel Kantha Temple, Kalinjar*

The first gateway guarding the steep ascent to Kalinjar is the Alamgir Darwaza. The Ganesha Darwaza follows. Strategically placed, it is the strongest of the gates, defended by bastions on either side. The other gates are the Chandi, Budh-bhadr, Hanuman and Lal *darwazas*. The Budh-bhadr Darwaza, also called the Swarg-rohan or heaven-ascending gate, refers to the auspicious planet Mars. Along the incline are the Hanuman and Bhairon *kunds*. The seventh and last gate, the Bara Darwaza, is elaborately inscribed and leads onto the flat hilltop.

Much has survived in Kalinjar despite Islamic iconoclasm and Victorian prudishness — indeed, nineteenth century Europeans strained to appreciate the amalgam of philosophy in the *yonis* and *lingams*. The sculpture and rock-writings in the fort articulate an all-encompassing culture, including that of the Gupta and Chandella periods.

◄ *Dark blue stone lingam with silver eyes at Neel Kantha Temple*

The Neel Kantha temple, containing a dark blue stone *lingam* with silver eyes, has been the main object of worship at Kalinjar for well over a millennium. Shiva in the phallic form depicting procreation is at the centre. The pavilion outside is classic Chandella architecture, with exquisite chiselling on granite pillars and mouldings, arches and capitals. A large black stone inside the temple indulges in bombastic praise of Parmardideva.

A giant Mahasadashiva is hewn within a recess in the rock. The polished figure rises to a height of twenty-four feet. The deity, with eighteen arms is ornamented with a garland of skulls. It is bedecked by snake armlets and a serpent drapes its neck. Close to this form of Shiva — the destroyer — is a statue of Kali, the stone rendered smooth and shining by an overhead trickle of water.

▲ *The Kot Tirth is a pilgrimage site where thousands take a dip*

Kalinjar is reputed to have suffered a water crunch at crucial times. However, on the other hand, there are a number of tanks and springs in the fort in evidence — seemingly, a perennial source of water. The Patal Ganga, or the underground Ganges, is a large cavern cut in the rock. The water is deep and clear. The Pandu *kund*, named after the Pandavas, is a shallow circular basin into which water trickles from rock crevices. An inscription, in Gupta Brahmi, dates the basin to the fifth century.

Among the profusion of tanks is the Sita *kund*; the Mrig *dhara* or the deer spring, which is a fountain of cool water; and the Bhuriya *tal* which is said to have healing powers. The Kot Tirth is a holy spot with a large tank and several *ghats* in which thousands take a dip on festive days. Legend says that the Chandella king, Kirtivarman, was cured of leprosy after bathing in the Kot Tirth.

◄ *Underground water tanks provided a perennial supply of water*

Scattered in the fort are sati memorials: sculptures of a woman's forearm covered with bracelets, the palm held open. Also carved in the stone, are the sun and moon, symbolising immortality which the ritual of sati was tragically believed to bring. The bangles and bracelets on the woman's forearm is a symbol for the belief that a woman who immolated herself on her husband's pyre was not considered to be a widow. Having accompanied her husband in death, the bangles and bracelets remained intact.

The original Sati, to avenge an insult to her consort Shiva — he had not been invited to a *yajna* by her father Daksha — is believed to have used her innate powers to create a fire and consume herself before a divine assemblage. The mythology of Sati's regeneration as Parvati and

reunion with Shiva perpetuated. The terror of self-immolation was sought to be mitigated by the spurious social conditioning that sati bestowed sacredness. Governor-General Bentinck's Regulation XVII was a significant step towards eliminating sati.

Captain Sleeman, who accompanied the Governor-General in his tour through Bundelkhand, wrote in his account 'Suttee Tombs — Insalubrity of Deserted Fortresses' in *Rambles and Recollections* (1915, p 221) : 'The village stands upon a gentle swelling hill…there is a very unusual number of tombs built over the ashes of women who have burnt themselves with the remains of their husband…When I passed this place on horseback with Lord William Bentinck, he asked me what these tombs were, for he had not seen any of the kind before. When I told him what they were, he said not a word…'

At Kalinjar — as in Bundelkhand — consciousness is patterned by oracles, legend and fragments of history. Desolate pathways appear to be in wait for cavalcades, gilded elephants and standard-bearers. Monkeys swing lithely from overhanging tree boughs nudging the abandoned

▶ *Sati memorial at Kalinjar*

Sati pillars in Bundelkhand – (left to right) Orchha, Mahoba and Narwar

ramparts of Kalinjar. There is the hint of an anklet sound in the hush of the pavilions where Kirat Singh's daughter Durgavati grew up. And the swish of a *ghaghra*. It does not last. The musing continues, overtaken by silence.

A view from Kundar fort

SOME EXPLANATORY NOTES

Abul Fazl: b.1551, d.1602, chief counsellor, historiographer and trusted friend of the Mughal emperor, Akbar. Waylaid and assassinated by **Bir Singh Bundela**, a prince of Orchha, who later became ruler of the state.

Ain-i-Akbari: 'Institutes of Akbar', in three volumes, compiled by Abul Fazl and other authors. Is a survey of the Mughal empire, including departmental regulations, statistics and historical notes.

Akbar: b. 1542, d. 1605, main architect of the Mughal empire. Born in Amarkot, Sindh during adverse times — his father **Humayun** was fleeing **Sher Shah Sur** who had routed the Mughals and taken Delhi. Humayun was given asylum in Persia; he returned to Delhi in 1555 but died soon after from a fall. Akbar was versatile and successful in forging alliances with the Rajputs. Expanded territory and promoted all-round reforms, revenue administration and religious tolerance. Reign (1556–1605) coincided with England's **Elizabeth I** (1558–1603). Akbar's tomb is at Sikandra, Agra. He is referred to as Akbar the Great.

Alberuni: b.973, d.1048, scholar of wide interests in court of **Mahmud of Ghazni**. Proficient in Sanskrit. Surveyed Hindu philosophy, including the *Bhagvad Gita*. Visited India. Wrote his observations in the *Tarikhu'l Hind*.

Anglo-Maratha Wars: Series of wars commencing in 1775. In initial stages, Maratha confederacy convincingly prevailed upon the British. Mahadji Scindia's death, the entry of Governor-General **Marquess Wellesley** (1798–1805), reversals in battlefield and political developments turned the tables. Governor-General **Lord Hastings** (1812–23) wrote the final chapter: the Peshwa's dominions were annexed and he was exiled to Bithoor (near Kanpur) in 1818. **Nana Sahib**, leader of the 1857–58 uprising, was the adopted son of the exiled Peshwa.

Aurangzeb: b.1618, d.1707, son and successor of **Shahjehan**, his ascent followed a bloody war of succession (1657–59). His reign (1658–1707) saw expansion in the Deccan. He was puritanical and in recurring conflict with the Marathas under **Shivaji** and his successors. Struggles with the Rajputs, Jats and Bundelas contributed to depletion of Mughal strength, leading to empire's decline and rise of the Marathas in eighteenth century. His undoing was in the Deccan. Buried in Khuldabad near Daulatabad fort (Aurangabad).

Babar: b.1483, d.1530, established Mughal rule by defeating the Delhi Sultan, **Ibrahim Lodi**, at Panipat in 1526. A Chaghtai Turk, Babar was descended from **Timur** on his father's side and, on his mother's side, from **Chinghiz Khan**. Babar inherited Ferghana, now in Uzbegistan An accomplished general, Babar was also a writer and poet; he wrote his memoirs in Turki. Artillery was central to Babar's military strategies. He worsted the Rajput confederacy under **Maharana Sanga** of Chittor. Died in Agra. Buried in Kabul.

Baji Rao I: b.1700, d.1741, Maratha Peshwa (1720–41) (hereditary minister heading Maratha confederacy). Saw steep Mughal decline. Statesman and soldier, he augmented troop mobility, cavalry and arms. Attained dominance over Malwa, Gujarat and the Deccan. Subdued the Rajputs and Portuguese. On **Chhatrasal**'s entreaties, defeated Mughal *subehdar* **Bangash Khan** of Farrukhabad in Bundelkhand — in return, Peshwa was presented with the beautiful **Mastani** and one-third of Chhatrasal's possessions.

Baptiste and the French in India: Colonel Jean Baptiste Filose is illustrative of the Frenchmen who were available for assisting the Indian princes towards the latter half of the eighteenth century, when the struggle against the British grew intense. French political aspirations had already collapsed in India. The French settlements were occupied by the British, but there were French soldiers under French control — in harness for employment. **Raymond** was available for the Nizam of Hyderabad, and **de Boigne** and **Perron** for the Scindia of Gwalior. Baptiste was a later entry — engaging in soldiering, adventurism and as an *agent provocateur*.

Bhishma: One of the most honoured figures of the epic Mahabharata. Dutiful son, who gave up marriage and the throne. Symbol of mature wisdom. Respected by both the warring sides: the Kauravas and Pandavas.

Bir Singh: Orchha ruler (1605–27). Cemented Bundela–Mughal relationship. Reign saw the flowering of distinctive Bundela architecture by blending Rajput and Mughal traditions, as illustrated in Orchha and Datia. When a prince, murdered **Akbar**'s chief counsellor **Abul Fazl** at the behest of Prince Salim. On Salim becoming emperor, he installed Bir Singh as the Orchha ruler. Orchha's court was enriched by the vivacious **Praveen Rai**, paramour of Bir Singh, and the court-poet **Keshav Das**.

Bundela Rising of 1842: A feudal revolt against the British by some discontented local chiefs in Bundelkhand who were unsettled by the establishment of British authority and loss of autonomy. The extent to which 1842 was a curtain raiser to 1857 in Bundelkhand is a matter of debate.

▲ *The Betwa at Deogarh*

Bundelkhand: The region includes the present districts of Banda, Chitrakut, Hamirpur, Jalaun, Jhansi, Lalitpur and Mahoba in Uttar Pradesh. The districts in Madhya Pradesh are Ashoknagar, Chhatarpur, Damoh, Datia, Panna, Sagar and Tikamgarh, and parts of Bhind, Guna, Gwalior, Satna and Shivpuri. The name of the region is associated with the Bundelas. In the pre-Bundela period, the region was known as Jajhauti — where the Jajhauti Brahmins lived.

Champat Rai: Bundela chieftain. Assisted Orchha's **Jujhar Singh** against the Mughals. Served Mughal prince **Dara Shikoh**, rival brother of Aurangzeb. Camp rivalries motivated Champat to switch to **Aurangzeb** whom he helped decisively in the Mughal succession. Made Mughal *mansabdar*; later revolted against Aurangzeb's bigotry. Pursued by **Sujan Singh Bundela** of Orchha, Champat Rai and wife **Lal Kunwar** took their lives in 1661. Their son was **Chhatrasal**.

Chhatrasal: b.1649, d.1731, he challenged the Mughals, extended reach and attained significant autonomy. Earlier served the Mughals. Role model was **Shivaji**, who advised Chhatrasal to campaign in his own territory against the Mughals. Took Kalinjar and Dhamoni; plundered Malwa. Patronised the liberal Pranami religious sect of Hinduism. Sought Maratha help against Mughals; in return, willed one-third of his possessions to Peshwa **Baji Rao I** — which introduced Maratha presence in Bundelkhand.

Cunningham, Alexander: British army engineer (b.1814, d.1893); retired in 1861 as Major General, and then became first Director of Indian Archaeological Survey. Excavated many sites in India, including Sanchi, Sarnath, as well as in Bundelkhand. Wrote illuminating reports, of permanent value.

Deccan: The area lying to the south of the river Narmada and north of the rivers, Krishna and Tungabhadra.

Gondwana: Gond kingdom, south of Bundelkhand, extinguished in 1564 by Akbar. Gonds were among the original inhabitants of the region. The regent-queen **Durgavati** governed Gondwana for her son **Bir Narayan**. In final battle against Mughals, a wounded Durgavati stabbed herself to death to avoid capture. Bir Narayan was slain when the Gond fort of Chauragarh fell to the Mughals. Durgavati was a Chandel, daughter of **Kirat Singh** who held Kalinjar before its capture in 1545 by Sultan **Sher Shah Sur**.

Hiuen Tsang: Chinese sage, traveller and chronicler, also known as Yuan Chwang. Meticulously recorded life in India during the reign of **Harshavardhana** (606–647). Spent eight years (635–643) in Harsha's kingdom.

Holkar: Maratha rulers of **Indore. Malhar Rao Holkar**, a distinguished military commander, was the first chief, assigned (1729) by Peshwa Baji Rao I to manage Malwa and administer lands to maintain the Maratha troops. Annexed much territory in Bundelkhand in 1735.

Jehangir: b. 1569, d.1627, son and successor of **Akbar** from emperor's Rajput Kachhwaha wife from Amber. Named **Salim** after Shaikh Salim Chishti of Sikri; renamed Jehangir on ascending throne in 1605. Contributed to empire's stability. Friend of **Bir Singh Bundela** of Orchha. Art connoisseur. Reputation for justice. Given to good living, intemperate drinking and bouts of cruelty. Dependent on wife Empress **Nur Jehan**, daughter of revenue minister **Ghiyas Beg**, referred to as Itimad-ud-daula, a Persian. Buried in Lahore.

Kalachuris: A dynasty of early times in Central India, which developed in the Narmada valley. Their era is believed to commence from 248 AD, when they came into possession of Kalinjar. The dynasty revived in the ninth century, and lasted till the eleventh.

Kannauj: Ancient town on the Ganges. Called Kanogiza by the Roman historian, Ptolemy. Capital of Harshvardhana's empire in the seventh century. Later became capital of the Pratiharas in the eighth century. Declined after its conquest by Mahmud of Ghazni in the eleventh century. Today, an important market for *ittar*, rose water and tobacco.

Kautilya: Also known as Chanakya. A Brahmin and astute strategist, known for uncompromising perseverance. His *Arthashastra* is a classic treatise on statecraft and administrative institutions. Given credit for overthrowing the Nandas and enthroning **Chandragupta Maurya** (322–298 BC).

Keshav Das: b.1555, d.1617, a Sanadhya Misra, is regarded as one of the first great writers on the art of poetry. Adorned Orchha's court. Helped develop the Bundela–Mughal relationship. Close to **Birbal**, one of the 'nine jewels' in Akbar's court. Has written valuable studies on poetical composition and prosody. Keshav's verse-systematisation had a pupil in **Praveen Rai:** she resorted to verse, when rebuffing Jehangir's overtures. Keshav's works include *Vigyan Gita, Kavi Priya* and *Ram Chandrika*.

Lakshmi Bai: Born at Benaras to Bhagirathi Bai — date of birth uncertain, maybe 1827. Father **Moropant Tambe** was retainer of **Chimanji Appa**, brother of the exiled Peshwa **Baji Rao II**. Lakshmi Bai moved with father to Bithoor (near Kanpur), where the Peshwa lived in exile with

▶ *Entrance to Jehangir Mahal, built by Bir Singh Bundela of Orchha*

his adopted son Nana Sahib. Married in 1842 to the Raja of Jhansi, a widower. In 1851, Lakshmi Bai had a son who did not survive. Subsequently, a boy, Damodar Rao, was adopted. Adoption was not recognised by the British. On the Raja's death in 1853, Jhansi stood annexed.

Lutyens, Edwin: b.1869, d.1944, premier architect, designed New Delhi. Planned a new imperial capital — with magnificent buildings, vistas and avenues — in the context of the shifting of the capital from Calcutta to Delhi in 1911. Incorporated historical styles.

Mahmud of Ghazni: b.971, d.1030, ascended in 997; kingdom comprised present Afghanistan and Khorasan in eastern Persia. Led numerous expeditions to India. Halted at Kalinjar by the Chandellas. Looted Somnath on Kathiawar coast. Islamic zealot. Said to have maintained Hindu soldiers who spearheaded victory over the Turks of Transoxiana. Suppressed the Seljuk Turks to occupy western Persia. Firdaus was one of his court poets.

Marathas: Major political force under **Shivaji** (1628-80), crowned Chhatrapati in 1674. Military strength came from a chain of forts, devoted soldiering and a muscular navy. Guerrilla tactics gave way to artillery and cavalry. Shivaji's dynasty overshadowed by the Peshwa — minister of the Maratha confederacy — which became a hereditary position. Confederacy included **Scindia** of Gwalior, **Holkar** of Indore, **Gaekwar** of Baroda and **Bhonsle** of Nagpur. Eighteenth century was dominated by Marathas. Sought to regain power in 1857, under **Nana Sahib**, adopted son of the exiled Peshwa **Baji Rao II**.

Mastani: beautiful and talented mistress of Peshwa **Baji Rao I**. Presented by a grateful Chhatrasal to the Peshwa for helping drive out the Mughal *subehdar* **Bangash Khan** from Bundelkhand. Mastani bore (1734) the Peshwa a son, **Shamsher Bahadur**, who died of wounds received in the third battle of Panipat (1761). **Ali Bahadur**, the Nawab of Banda (killed at Kalinjar, 1802), was the son of Shamsher Bahadur.

Mughals: Dynasty founded (1526) in India by **Babar**. Ancestral seat in Central Asia. Succeeded (1530) by **Humayun**, deposed (1540) by the Afghan Sher Shah Sur. Humayun restored (1555) Mughal rule. Son, **Akbar** the Great (1556–1605), established the empire. Subsequent three emperors, **Jehangir** (1605–27), **Shahjehan** (1628–58) and **Aurangzeb** (1658–1707) also recognised as great Mughal rulers. Rapid decline followed Aurangzeb's rule. **Bahadur Shah Zafar** was last in line: he was exiled to Rangoon by the British after the 1857 uprising.

Nana Sahib: b.1824, d. not known. Adopted by the exiled Peshwa **Baji Rao II** in 1827. Lived in Bithoor near Kanpur. Heir-presumptive to the throne. Well educated. At ease with Europeans.

▲ *Painting in the Datia School of Art style*

After seizing Kanpur, Nana Sahib declared himself Peshwa, calling for an end to British power in India. After the uprising, escaped to Nepal. Nothing known subsequently.

Panipat: There were three decisive battles on the Panipat plains, north of Delhi. The first battle (1526) saw Babar, with his artillery, trouncing the much larger army of the Delhi Sultanate led by **Ibrahim Lodi**. Mughal rule commenced. The second battle (1556) was due to Humayun's sudden death, the tenuousness of Mughal rule and the ambitions of the **Sur Afghans**. The Mughals under Akbar — still in his early teens — fought **Hemu**, a Hindu from Rewari and minister with the Surs. The Mughals triumphed. The third battle (1761) saw the Peshwa **Balaji Baji Rao** defeated by **Ahmad Shah Abdali** of Afghanistan, a significant setback to Maratha ambitions.

Paramaras: Rajput dynasty of Malwa from the ninth to thirteenth century. Ruled from Dhar. Prominent king was Raja Bhoja (1018–1060).

Peshwa: Headed the Maratha confederacy. Originally, the leading minister or prime minister. Became hereditary. Successively competent Peshwas in the first half of the eighteenth century ensured the sustenance of **Shivaji's** dominions, its transition into a powerful confederacy and the nurturing of Maratha identity. The direct descendant of Shivaji became a nominal head. Real power came to rest with the Peshwa — a major factor behind Maratha dominance of eighteenth-century India. The third battle of Panipat was a blow to the Peshwa's power.

Pratiharas: Rajput dynasty of northern India from the eighth to eleventh century. The capital was **Kannauj**, captured in 1018–19 by **Mahmud of Ghazni**.

Puranas: Religious stories, are popular compilations of religion, mythology and philosophy. Help understand the higher truths of life and society. Supplement the Vedas and believed to date from about 600 BC to 500 AD. There are eighteen Puranas. Useful in constructing the early political history of the country.

Rashtrakutas: The dynasty ruled the Deccan and neighbouring areas from the seventh to the tenth century.

Rousselet, Louis: French traveller and surveyor. Wrote *L'Inde des Rajahs* ('India and its Native Princes') after travelling extensively in India during 1863–68. The book was published in 1875, with an English translation the following year.

Scindia: Prominent chiefs of the Peshwa. The Scindias' rise was accelerated by the decline of the Peshwa following the Panipat debacle (1761). Became arbiter and protector of the Mughals. In return, Mughal emperor sanctioned executive authority. **Mahadji Scindia**, greatest of the line, took Delhi's Red Fort by assault. Subdued the Pathans and Rajput princes. Gwalior became the Scindia's base. Used the Savoyard, Count **Benoit de Boigne**, to modernise his armies. Another Frenchman, **Jean Baptiste Filoise**, led the Scindia's armies to many successes in Bundelkhand.

Shahjehan: b.1592, d.1666, son and successor of **Jehangir**; mother was a Rajput. Named **Khurram**, becoming Shahjehan on ascending the throne. Married in 1612 to **Arjumand Bano** or **Mumtaz Mahal**, daughter of the nobleman **Asaf Khan**, brother of **Itimad-ud-daula** (father of Nur Jehan). Diligent ruler (1628–58). Built Taj Mahal — mausoleum for Mumtaz Mahal (d. 1631). Imprisoned by his son and successor **Aurangzeb** in the last years of his life. Buried in the Taj Mahal, Agra alongside his wife.

Sher Shah Sur: Afghan of the Sur tribe, ruled Delhi (1540–45) after deposing the Mughal, **Humayun**. Earlier, in **Babar's** service, fought in Chanderi (1528). Fell out with the Mughals and united the Afghans against them. With Bihar as base, took Bengal. Seized Chunar fort; married commandant's widow. Forced Mughals into exile (1540–55) after defeating **Humayun** at Chausa (1539) and Kannauj (1540). Reformed revenue administration. Built roads, including the original Grand Trunk Road, now named after him. Killed at Kalinjar. Buried at Sasaram, Bihar.

Sleeman, William Henry: b.1788, d.1856; Bengal Army, appointed (1835) General

Superintendent of the Operations for the Suppression of Thuggee, headquartered at Jabalpur. Sleeman was gazetted as Captain in 1825, Major in 1837; he retired as a Major-General. Married Amelie Josephine, daughter of a French Revolution émigré. Wrote *Rambles and Recollections of an Indian Official*, which describes his tours. Escaped assassination attempt (1842) at Jhansi, and other attempts when Resident at Lucknow (1848–54). Experiences profiled in *Journey through the Kingdom of Oudh*. Died on board the *Monarch*, on his way home. Buried at sea.

Sultanate: The Turko-Afghan Sultanate of Delhi (1206–1526) saw the following dynasties: **Slave** (1206–1290), **Khilji** (1290–1320), **Tughlak** (1320–1414), **Sayyid** (1414–51) and **Lodi** (1451–1526). In its formative years, the Sultanate led to consolidation of Muslim power in northern India. Southward expansion reached maximum extent under **Ala-ud-din Khilji** (1296–1316). Fortunes fluctuated, including steep decline after **Timur's invasion** (1398). Babar defeated the Sultanate armies at Panipat (1526) to set up Mughal rule in Delhi.

Tatya Tope: b.1813, d. 1859. Father was a nobleman in court of the last Peshwa, **Baji Rao II.** Tatya's father accompanied, with family, the in-exile Peshwa to Bithoor. Primarily responsible for establishing **Nana Sahib**'s authority as the head of the revolutionaries. Daring leader. A central figure in Bundelkhand. After the events of 1857–58, continued to perplex the British. Betrayed to his British captors by a friend, **Man Singh of Narwar**. Tried and hanged.

Thuggee: Hereditary cult; members known as thugs. Worshipped goddess Kali. Engaged in large-scale robbery and murder by strangulation. Sleeman is widely regarded as chief architect and enforcer of the anti-thugee operations.

Tod, James: b.1782, d.1835; wrote *The Annals and Antiquities of Rajpootana*, monumental work on legends, history and social customs of the Rajputs. Appointed political agent for the states of western Rajputana. Joined the Bengal army as a cadet in 1799, led expeditions against the Pindaris (1814–15), while commanding the escort attached to the Scindia (1812–17). Returned to England in 1823.

Vedas: The primary texts of Hinduism. There are four Vedas: the Rig Veda, Sama Veda, Yajur Veda and Atharva Veda. The Vedas have influenced Buddhism, Jainism and Sikhism. The Rig Veda, the most ancient, is believed to be of around 1500 BC, codified about 600 BC, and put into writing sometime after 300 BC. The Upanishads are the continuation of Vedic philosophy.

❖

▲ *Rock-cut sculptures at Kalinjar*

SELECTED DATES

REFERENCES IN CHRONOLOGICAL ORDER

BC

2500–1500	Indus Valley Civilisation
1000–800	Epic India: Ramayana and Mahabharata
Sixth century	Chedi presence in Bundelkhand
563–483	Siddhartha Gautam, founder of Buddhism
537–467	Mahavira, founder of Jainism
Fifth–fourth century	Nanda dynasty
321–184 BC	Maurya dynasty

274–237 BC	Reign of Ashoka the Great
184–72 BC	Sunga dynasty

AD

First–second century	Kushana dynasty
Third century (248–249)	Kalachuris (descended from Chedis) occupy Kalinjar
Third–fourth century	Naga dynasty; Narwar — fortified settlement
320–late sixth century	Gupta dynasty
330–380	Reign of Samudragupta
Late fifth century	Huna invasions
Early sixth century	Deogarh's Dasavatara temple (Gupta period)
Seventh–eighth century	Gond chieftainships in Bundelkhand
606–647	Reign of Harsha Vardhana
641–642	Hiuen Tsang in Bundelkhand; in India from 635–643
660–974	Rashtrakuta dynasty of the Deccan
725–1018	Pratihara dynasty of Kannauj
831–1300s	Chandella dynasty
900–1200	Khajuraho temples built by Chandellas
940	Chandellas take Kalinjar from Rashtrakutas
978	Chandellas assist Lahore against Subuktagin of Ghazni
997–1030	Reign of Mahmud of Ghazni
1001	Chandellas assist Lahore against Mahmud of Ghazni
1019	Kalinjar: first expedition of Mahmud of Ghazni
1021	Mahoba-Kannauj policy conflict; Kannauj king killed
1022	Mahmud of Ghazni attacks Kalinjar for the second time
1182	Prithviraj Chauhan of Delhi defeats Chandellas
1192	Prithviraj slain by Muhammad Ghori

Thirteenth century	Chandella decline; rise of Khangars; later, of the Bundelas
1203	Kalinjar and Mahoba seized by Qutub-ud-din Aibak
1206	Aibak establishes Delhi Sultanate
1206–1290	Slave dynasty in Delhi
1251	Balban ravages Narwar and Chanderi
1290–1320	Khilji dynasty in Delhi
1309	Ala-ud-din Khilji devastates Bundelkhand
1320–1414	Tughlak dynasty in Delhi
1335	Ibn Batutah visits Khajuraho, Narwar and Chanderi
1398	Timur's invasion of India
1414–1450	Sayyid dynasty in Delhi
1436–1469	Malwa's Mahmud Khilji; ascendant over Chanderi
1450–1526	Lodi dynasty in Delhi
1526	Sultanate extinguished, Babar's Mughal rule begins
1528	Babar takes Chanderi
1530	Babar dies, succeeded by Humayun
1531	Bundelas establish capital at Orchha
1540	Humayun deposed, in exile from 1540 to 1555
1540–1545	Reign of Sher Shah Sur
1545	Kalinjar taken by Sher Shah Sur; succumbs to wounds
1555	Humayun restores Mughal rule, dies soon after
1555–1617	Keshav Das, leading light of Hindi poetry, at Orchha
1556–1605	Reign of Emperor Akbar
1564	Durgavati (last Chandel vestige) of Gondwana killed
1602	Murder of Abul Fazl by Bir Singh Bundela

1605–1627	Reign of Emperor Jehangir
1605–1627	Reign of Bir Singh, ruler of Orchha
1626	Datia invested by Bir Singh on son Bhagwan Rao
1628–1680	Chhatrapati Shivaji
1628–1657	Reign of Emperor Shahjehan
1635	Shahjehan visits Orchha; torches buildings
1649–1731	Chhatrasal Bundela
1658–1707	Reign of Emperor Aurangzeb
1661	Champat Rai (Chhatrasal's father) stabs himself to death
Eighteenth century	Decline of the Mughal rule
1720–1741	Administration of Baji Rao I — Maratha Peshwa
1720–1729	Bundela–Bangash Khan (Mughal *subehdar*) war
1729	Marathas enter Bundelkhand on Chhatrasal's entreaty
1742	Marathas appoint *subehdar* in Jhansi
1759–1806	Reign of Shah Alam, Mughal 'emperor'; blinded 1788
1761	Third Battle of Panipat — setback for Marathas
1818	Peshwa exiled — aftermath of Anglo-Maratha Wars
1828	W.R. Pogson's *A History of the Boondelas* published
1828–1835	Bentinck is Governor-General; visits Jhansi in 1832
1835–1842	W.H. Sleeman's interface with Bundelkhand
1848–1856	Dalhousie is Governor-General; enforces Doctrine of Lapse
1853	Jhansi 'lapses' into British India
1857	Outbreak of the Great Rebellion
1858	Rani Lakshmi Bai of Jhansi killed in battle
1859	Tatya Tope hanged

GLOSSARY

Acharya: learned and respected teacher

Akshaya tritiya: that which never diminishes; a very auspicious day

Alaap: overture

Alha: chivalrous song (of Bundelkhand); derived from the Banaphar youths Alha and Udal

Ambika: female figurines

Antarala: vestibule

Apsara: celestial dancing girl

Aradhana mudra: position of power or worship

Ashta shakti: eight goddesses

Avatara: incarnation

Baithak: reception or sitting place

Bala hissar: inner citadel

Baoli: a large well or water storage

Bar: banyan tree

Bazaar: market place

Begum: a woman of high rank

Bhabhi: elder brother's wife

Bhakti: devotion

Bhanja: sister's son

Bhawani Shankar: reference to Shiva

Bigha: a measure of area, of great variation, but never exceeding an acre

Boond: drop

Chandravanshi: descendant of the moon

Charan: foot (respectful connotation)

Chhatri: memorial canopy

▼ *Jauhar memorial, Chanderi*

Darbar: court

Dargah: the tomb of a Muslim saint, a Muslim shrine

Darul Islam: domain of Islam

Darwaza: gateway or entrance

Dasavatara: ten incarnations

Devi: Goddess

Devta: deity

Dhak: tree variety

Dharmashala: resting place for travellers

Dhobi: washerman

Dholak: a percussion instrument played during joyous occasions

Diwankhana: hall of public audience

Doab: between two rivers; in the present context, between the Ganges and the Yamuna in the Indo-Gangetic plains

Durbar: royal court of assembly

Fakir: a holy man

Gaja: elephant

Gandharvas: celestial musicians of Lord Indra

Garbhgraha: the interior and most sacred part of a Hindu temple

Garh: fort

Garhi: small fort

Garuda: the king of birds, Garuda is Vishnu's vehicle

Ghaghra: flowing skirt worn by women in some parts of India

Ghat: landing place on river or earmarked bathing place

Ghati: valley

Ghazi: a Muslim fighter against infidels

Giridurga: hill forts

Gopis: female cowherd friends of Lord Krishna

Gotras: sects

Hardaul ka chabutra: Hardaul's platform

Hathi: elephant

Havan kunds: the urn or 'altar' for Vedic fire sacrifice rituals

Hawa Paur: windy gate

Hijras: eunuchs

Ittar: incense

Jagir: grant or liege holding

Jagirdars: holder of grant or liege

Jaldurga: water forts

Jal samadhi: the voluntary giving up of life in water

Jauhar: mass self-immolation

▼ *The ghat at Deogarh*

Jhainsi: reflection

Kadak Bijli: thunder-lightning

Kauri: shell

Kavi Priya: compilation of poems by Orchha's poet Keshav Das

Khillat: sword of honour

Khutba: direction from Islamic religious authority

Kiledar: keeper of fort, chief of fort

Kirtan: devotional rendition

Kund: water reservoir or pond

Kutcherry: court house

Lalatabimba: projecting image

Lingam: phallic emblem

Mahal: (1) palace, (2) administrative unit

Mahatirtha: higher level of Hindu pilgrim spot

Mahidurga: mud forts

Mahotsava: important festival or celebration

Manastambha: votive pillar

Mangal: auspicious time

Mansab: high military rank conferred by the Mughals

Mansabdar: high military officer performing civil functions

Manu: considered a law giver in Hindu tradition

Masnad: designated sitting place

Math: temple

Maund: a unit of weight used in India, having different values in different localities

Mithunas: dancing figures

◀ *Carvings of Pramathas and Mithunas, Deogarh*

Mujahid: a Muslim fighter — active for Islam

Mussalchees: grinder of spices

Naga: serpent

Nahar ghati: river valley

Nakara: kettle drum

Nawab: chief, generally a Muslim designation (e.g. Nawab of Oudh)

Paan: betel leaf

Pakhawaj: a percussion instrument

Panj hazari mansab: a 'mansab' (see above) of five thousand horses

Pargana: administrative unit

Patravallari: variety of creepers

Pradakshinapath: processional passage

Pramathas: dwarfish male figures

Pratimasarvo bhadrika: Jina image visible from all sides

Prithviraj Raso: Chand Bardai's ode to Prithviraj Chauhan

Pujari: priest

Purdah: protection from exposure

Purohit: priest and guiding light

Qawwalis: lively rendition, in metre, in Sufi tradition

▲ *Painting of Ras Lila on the walls of Rani Mahal, Orchha*

Raksha Bandhan: a festival in which brothers renew their 'agreement to protect' their sisters

Raj: rule

Rani: queen

Ras lila: drama or performance based on Lord Krishna, Radha and the gopis

Sadhu: ascetic

Sahastrakuta: pillar carved with a thousand Jina figures

Sal: tree-variety

Samadhi: cenotaph, resting place

Samtal: level

Sanad: grant

Sangam: confluence of rivers

Sarangi: string instrument

Sarkar: administrative unit

Sarod: string instrument

Shikar: hunt

Shikari: hunter

Shikhara: spire or tower

Smriti shastras: the Smritis are laws that guide individuals in their daily conduct. They are also called Dharma Shastras or laws of righteous conduct.

Subehdar: administrative head of a province

Surahi: a long-necked container to keep water cool

Suryavanshi: descendant of the sun

▲ *Sahastralingam near the Kot Tirth, Kalinjar*

▲ *A talao at Kalinjar*

Tal: a pond

Talao: a pond

Tandav: dance of Shiva

Tapasya: worship, penance

Tapasyasthana: place of worship / penance

Tendu: a tree variety, its leaves are rolled around tobacco ('bidi') and smoked

Tilak: religious marking on forehead

Tirth: place of pilgrimage

Tirthankara: Jain religious reformer

Tonga: horse-drawn carriage

Upadhyayas: philosopher, teacher

Urs: a minor pilgrimage

Vaisakhi: season, corresponds to April (time for harvesting winter crop)

Vahanas: vehicles, carriers of gods and goddesses

Vanadurga: forest forts

Vaishnava: sect that worships Lord Vishnu

Yagnavalkaya: a law-maker

Yoni: the symbol under which Shakti, or the personification of the female power in nature, is worshipped

Zenana: women's enclosed quarters

▼ *Kalinjar*

REFERENCES

Ansari, M.A. (1975) *European Travellers under the Mughals (1580-1627)*. Delhi, Idarah-i-Adabiyat-i-Delhi.

Beveridge, A.S. (2003) *Babur-Nama*. Low Price Publication.

Crooke, W. (1896) *The Native Races of India: The Tribes and Castes of the North-Western India*. London, Methuen & Co.

Cunningham, A. (1969) *Archaeological Survey of India Reports*, Vol. II. Varanasi and Delhi, Indological Book House.

Dow, A. (1973) *The History of Hindostan*. Vol. II. Today & Tomorrow's Printers & Publishers.

Durant, W. (1935) *The Story of Civilization, I: Our Oriental Heritage*, New York, Simon and Schuster

Edwardes, M. (1963) *Battles of the Indian Mutiny*. B.T. Batsford Ltd.

Government of Uttar Pradesh, Department of District Gazetteers. (1988) *Uttar Pradesh District Gazetteer of Banda*.

Government of Uttar Pradesh, Department of District Gazetteers. (1989) *Uttar Pradesh District Gazetteer of Hamirpur*

Haig, W. (1971) 'Sher Shah and the Sur Dynasty: The Return of Humayun' in *The Cambridge History of India, Mughal India*, Vol. IV, Delhi, S Chand & Co.

Hibbert, C. (1978) *The Great Mutiny India 1857*. Allen Lane, Penguin Books Ltd.

Luard, C.L. (1907) *Samthar State Gazetteer*, The Central India State Gazetteer Series

Pogson, W.R. (1974) *A History of the Boondelas*. Delhi, B.R. Publishing Corporation.

Publications Bureau, Information Department, Uttar Pradesh. (1959) *Freedom Struggle in Uttar Pradesh, Source-Material, Bundelkhand and Adjoining Territories 1857-59*. Vol. III.

Rousselet, L. (1983) *India and its Native Princes, Travels in Central India and in the Presidencies of Bombay and Bengal*. Delhi, B.R. Publishing Corporation.

Sleeman, W.H. (1915) *Rambles and Recollections of an Indian Official*. Oxford, Oxford University Press.

Smith, V.A. (2004) *The Oxford History of India*. 21st ed. Oxford, Oxford University Press.

Tod, J. (1978) *Annals and Antiquities of Rajasthan*. Vol. I. Delhi, M.N. Publishers.